22 November 1963

A Brief Guide to the JFK Assassination

Jeremy Bojczuk

Boxgrove Publishing

Published by Boxgrove Publishing

First edition: October 2014

ISBN: 978–0–9931003–0–7

Contents

Author's Note

Anyone who studies the JFK assassination is likely to be overwhelmed by the vast amount of contradictory evidence and the many incompatible interpretations that bedevil the subject. This book, which is a revised and expanded version of a series of articles on the http://22november1963.org.uk/ website, is intended to provide both beginners and experts with a concise, readable, objective and fully referenced account of the central issues.

It should be pointed out that this book has been written largely in UK English for a largely US-based audience. Standard UK spelling has been used, except when quoting documents that use American spelling. If you notice any spelling mistakes, please assume that they are deliberate, even though they may not be.

A handful of American words have been incorporated, mainly to avoid conflicts with quoted documents. Almost all non-American readers will know that an elevator is a lift, and should be able to work out that a line-up is an identification parade. One particular example of American usage was unavoidable. You cannot have a book about the JFK assassination without using the term 'sixth floor.' The sixth floor in an American building would normally be called the fifth floor in, among other places, the UK, Ireland and continental Europe, where the first floor is the one immediately above the ground floor. In this book, floors are counted in the American way.

The text is identical in the paperback and digital versions of this book, apart from a small number of trivial differences imposed by the two formats, mostly in the wording and numbering of the footnotes. Some references which can be given as hyperlinks in the ebook version have had to be stated explicitly in the paperback version. For typographical reasons, a handful of footnotes which benefit from appearing separately in the ebook have needed to be amalgamated in the paperback.

There is one important difference between the two versions. Thanks to the work of the people behind the Mary Ferrell Foundation website, the History Matters website, and the Assassination Archives and Research Center website, a very large proportion of the unclassified primary evidence in the JFK assassination is now available to anyone with an internet connection. The ebook version of this title includes links wherever possible to those primary and secondary sources that are available online. It is perhaps the first ebook on this subject to provide comprehensive access to the evidence in this way. The URLs, or web addresses, of all online sources cited in both versions of the book were checked between 1 July 2014 and 15 July 2014 and found to be correct. Like everything else on the web, of course, they are liable to change or disappear without notice.

Abbreviations

The following abbreviations are used:

ARRB Assassination Records and Review Board

CD Warren Commission Document (items not published in the 26 *WCHE* volumes but instead placed in the National Archives)

CE Warren Commission Exhibit (official exhibits included in the 26 volumes and, in a few cases, the *Warren Report*)

Church Committee Senate Select Committee to Study Governmental Operations with Respect to Intelligence Activities (chaired by Senator Frank Church)

DRE *Directorio Revolucionario Estudiantil* (Revolutionary Student Directorate, also known as the Cuban Student Directorate)

FPCC Fair Play for Cuba Committee

HSCA House Select Committee on Assassinations

HSCA *Appendix* *Investigation of the Assassination of President John F. Kennedy: Appendix to Hearings Before the Select Committee on Assassinations*, US Government Printing Office, 1979 (the 12 volumes of hearings, exhibits and staff reports relating to the JFK assassination; a further 12 volumes deal with the Martin Luther King assassination)

HSCA Report *Final Report of the Select Committee on Assassinations*, US Government Printing Office, 1979

Lopez Report *Oswald, the CIA and Mexico City* (HSCA staff report, withheld from the HSCA *Appendix* volumes and partially declassified by the ARRB in the 1990s)

NAA Neutron Activation Analysis

NARA National Archives and Records Administration

NSAM National Security Action Memorandum

RIF Record Identification Form (for documents at NARA)

Schweiker–Hart Report *Final Report of the Senate Select Committee to Study Governmental Operations with Respect to Intelligence Activities, Book V: The Investigation of the Assassination of President John F. Kennedy: Performance of Intelligence Agencies,* US Government Printing Office, 1976

TSBD Texas School Book Depository

Warren Commission The President's Commission on the Assassination of President John F. Kennedy

Warren Commission Hearings and Exhibits* or *WCHE *Hearings before the President's Commission on the Assassination of President John F. Kennedy,* US Government Printing Office, 1964 (in 26 volumes)

Warren Report* or *WR *Report of the President's Commission on the Assassination of President John F. Kennedy,* US Government Printing Office, 1964

List of Tables

1 Who Killed President Kennedy?

This short book is not going to give you the answer, but it will try to illustrate the best way to think about the question.

Much of the evidence in the JFK assassination is inconclusive and open to a variety of interpretations. There are, however, some basic, indisputable, uncontroversial facts. These facts suggest only two realistic solutions, both of which revolve around the role of Lee Harvey Oswald: either Oswald killed Kennedy, with or without associates, or he was set up in advance to take the blame.

On 22 November 1963, President John F. Kennedy was a passenger in a motorcade through the centre of Dallas, Texas. At about 12:30pm, the motorcade was in Dealey Plaza, just outside the downtown area, when several gunshots were fired.[1] Altogether, three people were injured. President Kennedy was wounded in the back and the throat, and, fatally, in the head.[2] The governor of Texas, John Connally, who was sitting directly in front of Kennedy, sustained three wounds: one bullet hit him in the back, destroyed four inches of one rib, punctured his right lung, and came out of the right side of his chest; his right wrist was shattered; and a fragment of a bullet was embedded in his left thigh.[3] James Tague, a spectator standing on Commerce Street, close to the railway bridge

1. The basic, uncontested facts of the JFK assassination can be found in the *Warren Report*, pp.1–5.
2. Lack of agreement about the exact location and nature of the president's wounds is the main reason why the assassination remains controversial. President Kennedy's autopsy was carried out poorly: his back and throat wounds were not dissected, and none of his wounds was measured or photographed with adequate precision; see Appendix A, The Medical Evidence, p.105 below.
3. For Governor Connally's chest wound, see *WCHE*, vol.4, p.104. For his wrist wound, see *ibid.*, pp.118–120.

known as the Triple Underpass, received a slight cut on the cheek from the impact of a bullet to the concrete curb near his feet.[4]

At the time of the shooting, the presidential limousine was heading west on Elm Street, and had just passed the Texas School Book Depository, which contained publishers' offices and a book warehouse. A window was half open at the eastern end of the sixth floor of the building.[5] Three empty bullet shells were discovered just inside this window. Elsewhere on the sixth floor, a rifle was discovered. Tests showed that those bullet shells had been fired from that rifle.[6]

The rifle had been purchased several months earlier by mail order. The name on the mail order coupon was a pseudonym known to have been used elsewhere by a man named Lee Harvey Oswald. The handwriting on the coupon matched Oswald's. The supplier had sent the rifle to a post office box rented by Oswald, who worked in the Texas School Book Depository and had legitimate access to the sixth floor. Oswald claimed to have been elsewhere at the time of the shooting, but there were no eye-witnesses to support his alibi.[7]

On the face of it, this is an open-and-shut case: Oswald did it. The only realistic alternative is that Oswald had been carefully framed in advance. The other, purely theoretical, solution, that another lone nut stumbled across Oswald's rifle and decided to take a few pot shots at the president, is too unlikely to be worth considering. Either Oswald did it, or he was set up.

4. James Tague's wound: *WR*, p.116.
5. This is the American definition of 'sixth floor'; in the UK it would be the fifth floor. All such references will use the American definition.
6. For the discovery of the bullet shells and the rifle, see e.g. *WCHE*, vol.6, pp.300–301. The bullet shells were matched to the rifle by Robert Frazier of the FBI: *WCHE*, vol.3, pp.421–428.
7. A photograph of the envelope and mail order coupon for the rifle: *WCHE*, vol.19, p.275. Identification of the handwriting as Oswald's: CE 2145, p.1 (*WCHE*, vol.24, p.759). For Oswald's use of post office boxes, see *WCHE*, vol.20, p.177. For Oswald's use of 'A. Hidell' as an alias, see p.76 below. For Oswald's alibi, see p.25 below. The man now universally known as Lee Harvey Oswald rarely used his middle name except in official documents; he usually called himself either Lee Oswald or, in the American fashion, Lee H. Oswald.

2 Investigating the Crime

The rifle and bullet shells found at the scene of the crime suggested very strongly that Lee Harvey Oswald had fired three shots at President Kennedy. Other evidence quickly emerged which indicated that he had not been the only gunman.

The Texas School Book Depository was behind Kennedy at the time of the shooting, but many of the closest eye-witnesses described one or more shots coming from the opposite direction. The earliest newspaper accounts mentioned several witnesses who claimed that shots originated from the western end of Dealey Plaza. Charles Brehm, who was standing very close to President Kennedy, "seemed to think the shots came from in front of or beside the President," according to the *Dallas Times Herald* on the evening of 22 November. The *Dallas Morning News* on 23 November reported that Ochus Campbell, the vice-president of the Texas School Book Depository Company, "says he ran toward a grassy knoll to the west of the building, where he thought the sniper had hidden." Mary Woodward, a journalist on the *Dallas Morning News*, was standing on the north side of Elm Street, about halfway between the TSBD and the knoll. She wrote in the next day's edition that "suddenly there was a horrible, ear-shattering noise coming from behind us and a little to the right." Altogether, around forty witnesses claimed to have heard shots from the general direction of the grassy knoll.[1]

The medical staff who gave emergency treatment to Kennedy considered his throat wound to be one of entrance, not exit, and described a substantial exit wound extending to the back of his

1. See Appendix C, Grassy Knoll Witnesses, p.127 below.

head. In a press conference given shortly after the president's death, Dr Malcolm Perry stated that "the wound appeared to be an entrance wound in the front of the throat; yes, that is correct."[2] The rear head wound is described in several of the accounts made by the medical staff immediately after the treatment. For example, Dr William Kemp Clark, professor of neurosurgery and the most senior doctor present, described "a large wound in the right occipital–parietal region." The parietal bones are on the sides of the skull; the occipital bone is at the back of the skull.[3]

This evidence of gunfire from the front was reported by newspapers, radio and television very soon after the assassination. Although governmental and media opinion settled on Lee Harvey Oswald as the only assassin, the early news reports caused a great deal of public scepticism of the lone–gunman explanation, both in the USA and abroad. Suspicion increased when Oswald was himself murdered two days later, while in police custody, by another lone gunman, a man with connections to organised crime.[4]

Public scepticism of the lone–gunman account was expressed as public distrust of the governmental and media institutions which promoted that account. A letter to J. Edgar Hoover, the director of the FBI, typified the response of many upstanding citizens to the two assassinations:

> Like most of the people in the nation, my mother and I are shocked, appalled, angered and hurt by the assassination of President Kennedy. After seeing the television presentation of the killing of his suspected murderer, we are convinced more than ever that President Kennedy was the victim of a horrible conspiracy.... May we suggest that you start with the Dallas police force who seem to have been extraordinarily lax in their protection of Oswald, who might eventually have talked. The presence of Rubenstein [Jack Ruby] and his apparent role of 'fall guy' appear too pat to go unnoticed.[5]

2. ARRB Medical Document 41, p.6.
3. CE 392 (*WCHE*, vol.17, pp.1–22). Dr Clark's comment is on p.3.
4. Jack Ruby's links to organised crime were glossed over by the Warren Commission but acknowledged by the House Select Committee on Assassinations in a 1000–page report: *HSCA Appendix*, vol.9, pp.125–1117.
5. FBI HQ JFK Assassination File, 62–109060–15.

Within hours of Oswald's murder, Hoover identified the need to restore public confidence in the institutions of law and order and government, and discussed a possible solution:

> The thing I am concerned about, and so is Mr Katzenbach [the deputy Attorney General], is having something issued so that we can convince the public that Oswald is the real assassin. Mr Katzenbach thinks that the President might appoint a Presidential Commission of three outstanding citizens to make a determination.[6]

In a memo written later that day, Nicholas Katzenbach made the case for establishing what became the Warren Commission:

> The public must be satisfied that Oswald was the assassin; that he did not have confederates who are still at large; and that the evidence was such that he would have been convicted at trial. Speculation about Oswald's motivation ought to be cut off, and we should have some basis for rebutting thought that this was a Communist conspiracy or (as the Iron Curtain press is saying) a right–wing conspiracy to blame it on the Communists. Unfortunately the facts on Oswald seem about too pat — too obvious (Marxist, Cuba, Russian wife, etc.). The Dallas police have put out statements on the Communist conspiracy theory, and it was they who were in charge when he was shot and thus silenced.[7]

Discussions had been held with other Washington insiders. Joe Alsop, a newspaper columnist, telephoned President Johnson on the morning of President Kennedy's funeral and mentioned that he had recently spoken about this subject with several influential people, including: Katzenbach; Dean Acheson, the former Secretary of State; Fred Friendly, the president of CBS; and Bill Moyers, an assistant to Johnson. Alsop encouraged Johnson to establish

6. *HSCA Appendix*, vol.3, p.472. For more about the political necessity of the lone–gunman explanation and the creation of the Warren Commission, see Chapter 7, "A Little Incident in Mexico City", p.57 below.
7. FBI HQ JFK Assassination File, 62–109060–18.

a commission, pointing out that "what I'm really honestly giving you is public relation[s] advice."[8]

One week after the assassination, President Johnson created the Warren Commission, which had the explicit purpose of convincing the general public that Oswald alone had killed President Kennedy. The Commission's report endorsed and expanded an earlier FBI report, and presented more evidence against Oswald to add to the bullet shells and rifle found in the Texas School Book Depository. Photographs were discovered of Oswald holding what appeared to be the same rifle. His wife admitted that he had owned the rifle, and that he had planned to kill the former vice–president, Richard Nixon. In addition to the shooting in Dealey Plaza, Oswald was held to have shot dead a policeman in a suburb of Dallas about forty minutes later, and to have attempted to assassinate a retired general in Dallas several months earlier.[9]

The *Warren Report* was issued in one volume in September 1964, and was immediately and widely praised in the print and broadcast media. More informed and disinterested voices, however, found it less convincing. The philosopher, Bertrand Russell, pointed out a fundamental problem with the Commission's approach:

> At the outset the Commission appointed six panels through which it would conduct its enquiry. They considered: What did Oswald do on November 22, 1963? What was Oswald's background? What did Oswald do in the U.S. Marine Corps, and in the Soviet Union? How did Ruby kill Oswald? What is Ruby's background? What efforts were taken to protect the President on November 22? This raises my fourth question: Why did the Warren Commission not establish a panel to deal with the question of who killed President Kennedy?[10]

8. Joe Alsop to Lyndon Johnson, White House Telephone Transcripts, 25 November 1963, 10:40am, LBJ Library, Austin, Texas.
9. Photographs of Oswald with a rifle: *WR*, p.126. Marina Oswald described the weapon found on the sixth floor of the Texas School Book Depository as "the fateful rifle of Lee Oswald": *WCHE*, vol.1, p.119. Oswald's intention to kill Richard Nixon: *WR*, pp.187–189. The killing of J.D. Tippit: *WR*, pp.156–175. The attempted assassination of General Edwin Walker: *WR*, pp.183–188.
10. Bertrand Russell, '16 Questions on the Assassination,' *Minority of One*, 6 September 1964, pp.6–8.

Two months later, once the reviews had appeared, the report's twenty–six volumes of hearings and exhibits were published. Although hundreds of thousands of copies of the *Warren Report* were issued in paperback to coincide with the publication of the official edition, public access to the documentary evidence was carefully rationed. Only 5000 copies of the complete supplementary volumes were printed, all in expensive hardback format. Much of the background material was not published at all, but placed in the National Archives. Other material was deemed to be dangerous to national security, and was ordered to be kept secret for 75 years. A series of law suits under the Freedom of Information Act enabled some of this material, such as the transcripts of the Commission's executive sessions, to be made public.

A number of citizens took the trouble to examine the supplementary volumes. They discovered that not only were most of the *Report*'s conclusions not strongly supported by the evidence it cited, but that in several instances its conclusions were actively contradicted by the evidence it cited. Although the earliest critical books were not widely or sympathetically reviewed in the press, they influenced the general public's growing scepticism of the lone–assassin explanation.[11]

Also unconvinced about the *Warren Report*'s conclusions were three of the seven Commissioners. The most vociferous objector, Senator Richard Russell, called a special meeting of the Commission just as the *Warren Report* was about to be sent to the printers. He set out his objections to the central part of the case against Oswald, and supplied two written statements to be added to the record. The need for the appearance of unanimity among the Commissioners ensured that Russell's objections were mentioned only obliquely in the final version of the *Warren Report*: "Governor Connally's testimony and certain other factors have given rise to some difference of opinion ... but there is no question in the mind of any member of the Commission that all the shots which caused the President's and Governor Connally's wounds were fired from the

11. The most influential of the early works criticising the *Warren Report* were: Harold Weisberg, *Whitewash: the Report on the Warren Report*, Weisberg, 1965; Sylvia Meagher, *Accessories After the Fact: the Warren Commission, the Authorities, and the Report*, Bobbs–Merrill, 1967; and Josiah Thompson, *Six Seconds in Dallas: A Micro–Study of the Kennedy Assassination*, Bernard Geis Associates, 1967.

sixth floor window of the Texas School Book Depository."[12] Later that day, Russell explained to President Johnson that "I couldn't sign it. And I said that Governor Connally testified directly to the contrary, and I'm not going to approve of that.... I tried my best to get in a dissent, but they'd come round and trade me out of it."[13] Senator Russell was displeased when a researcher informed him several years later that no record of his objections had been preserved; the official minutes of the Warren Commission's final meeting, at which a stenographer was present, contained neither the usual *verbatim* transcript nor Russell's two written statements.[14]

Over time, as more research was undertaken, and as more and more previously classified documents became available to researchers, public trust in the Warren Commission's conclusions and objectivity diminished even further. In response to the increasing number of critical books and films, an internal CIA memo of 1967 pointed out that "46% of the American public did not think that Oswald acted alone," and regretted that "this trend of opinion is a matter of concern to the US government, including our organization.... Efforts to impugn [the Warren Commissioners'] rectitude and wisdom tend to cast doubt on the whole leadership of American society." The document went on to propose that the CIA ought to "discuss the publicity problem with liaison and friendly elite contact (especially politicians and editors) ... employ propaganda assets to ... refute the attacks of the critics. Book reviews and feature articles are particularly appropriate for this purpose."[15] If there was a deliberate attempt to change or control public opinion, it has not been entirely successful. Although the public continues to tolerate established political institutions, only a small minority has been convinced by the news media's promotion of the lone–assassin hypothesis. Since the 1970s, polls have consistently claimed that around three–quarters of the US population suspect that the JFK assassination was the result of a conspiracy of one

12. *WR*, p.19.
13. Lyndon Johnson to Richard Russell, White House Telephone Transcripts, 18 September 1964, LBJ Library, Austin, Texas.
14. Minutes of Warren Commission Executive Session, 18 September 1964. For a full treatment of Richard Russell's objections, see Gerald D. McKnight, *Breach of Trust: How the Warren Commission Failed the Nation and Why*, University Press of Kansas, 2005, pp.282–297.
15. CIA document 1035–960: NARA RIF no. 104–10009–10022.

sort or another. The figure has rarely gone below 70%, and in 1976 and 2001 no fewer than 81% of those surveyed rejected the Warrren Commission's verdict.[16]

Altogether, nine official bodies have looked into various aspects of the JFK assassination. Two of these investigations coincided with the activities of the Warren Commission. Shortly after the formation of the Commission, the FBI produced a lengthy but very superficial report, which failed to mention all of the wounds and spent only one page on the details of the assassination. On 25 November, the attorney general of Texas had set up a court of inquiry. Activity behind the scenes in Washington ensured that the Texan inquiry was in effect closed down and absorbed into the Warren Commission. The court of inquiry produced a token 20–page report in October 1964 which repeated the Commission's conclusions.

Four years later, the Attorney General, Ramsey Clark, assembled a group of four doctors to deal with some of the troublesome aspects of the medical evidence, such as the observation by the pathologists at the autopsy that President Kennedy's skull contained an entry wound that was too low to have been the result of a shot fired from the sixth floor of the TSBD. The Clark Panel, none of whose members had examined the corpse, moved the entrance wound up by four inches or ten centimetres, thereby allowing a hypothetical lone gunman to have fired the fatal shot from the sixth floor. At around the same time, a criminal investigation was begun into a New Orleans businessman, Clay Shaw, who was accused of participation in the assassination. He stood trial in 1969, and was rapidly acquitted.

The Rockefeller Commission, which was set up in 1975 to investigate the activities of the CIA within the US, touched on the assassination. The television broadcast that year of the Zapruder film had forced the Rockefeller Commission to make the first official acknowledgement that Kennedy's head had moved sharply backwards as a result of the fatal shot, a fact which the *Warren*

16. Sheldon Appleton, 'The Mystery of the Kennedy Assassination: What the American Public Believes,' *The Public Perspective*, October/November 1998, pp.13–17, available at http://www.ropercenter.uconn.edu/public-perspective/ppscan/96/96013.pdf (PDF: 7.2 MB). For the 2001 opinion poll, see Darren K. Carlson, 'Most Americans Believe Oswald Conspired With Others to Kill JFK,' at http://www.gallup.com/poll/1813/most-americans-believe-oswald-conspired-others-kill-jfk.aspx.

Report had for some reason neglected to mention. The following year, the Church Committee reported on the illegal gathering of information by the CIA and the FBI, and was very critical of the role of both agencies in withholding information from the Warren Commission.

The House Select Committee on Assassinations in 1977–78 also criticised the CIA and the FBI, as well as the Secret Service and the Warren Commission itself, and concluded that "President John F. Kennedy was probably killed as a result of a conspiracy."[17]

The Assassination Records Review Board, which operated between 1992 and 1998, did not investigate the facts of the assassination, but did interview several interested parties. It was set up to enable the release to the public of the huge numbers of secret records relating to the assassination, including those on which the HSCA's conclusions were based. Perhaps the ARRB's most important achievements were the belated publication of the HSCA's *Lopez Report*, which dealt with the activities of Lee Oswald in Mexico City a few weeks before the assassination, and the revelation that George Joannides, the CIA officer who acted as a liaison between the Agency and the HSCA, had been personally involved in 1963 with a CIA–funded anti–Castro organisation that had interacted with Oswald in New Orleans and had helped him to create a political persona that would be used against him after the assassination.

Three other official investigations were proposed but did not come into existence. Shortly after the assassination, members of each House suggested setting up their own investigations. Both groups were persuaded that the Warren Commission's investigation would be more authoritative if it had no competitors. In 1967, Theodore Kupferman, a Republican Congressman, responded to the increasing public criticisms of the Warren Commission by proposing that a committee should review the work of the Commission. His proposal too was unsuccessful.[18]

The most prominent of these later investigations was that of the House Select Committee on Assassinations, although neither the public nor the media, for differing reasons, fully accepted its

17. *HSCA Report*, p.3.

18. For Rep. Kupferman's official correspondence regarding his proposal, see Thompson, *op. cit.*, pp.285–291.

interpretation of the assassination: that Oswald had been the assassin, and that an unidentified person had also fired a shot, which missed. A recording had come to light of a police radio broadcast that appeared to contain evidence of a fourth gunshot. Acoustic tests indicated that the evidence was credible and that the fourth shot was fired from the infamous grassy knoll at the north–west corner of Dealey Plaza. The HSCA was unable to dispose of this evidence before its report was due to be published, and so was obliged to suggest the existence of a third, albeit unsuccessful, lone nut in addition to Oswald and Ruby. The acoustical evidence is technical, and its interpretation is disputed. In what may count as a tenth official inquiry into aspects of the assassination, the Department of Justice sponsored the National Research Council to produce a report questioning the HSCA's interpretation of the acoustical evidence.[19]

The HSCA's case against Oswald largely followed that of the Warren Commission. Although the Commission had successfully refuted one or two of the earliest and more improbable conspiracy theories, neither it nor the Select Committee was able to provide a convincing account of exactly how Lee Harvey Oswald killed President Kennedy.

19. National Research Council, *Report of the Committee on Ballistic Acoustics*, report no. PB83–218461, 1982; available at http://www.nap.edu/catalog.php?record_id=10264 (PDF: 3.1 MB). The HSCA's treatment of the acoustical evidence is in *HSCA Appendix*, vol.8. For the case in favour of a shot from the grassy knoll, see D.B. Thomas, 'Echo Correlation Analysis and the Acoustic Evidence in the Kennedy Assassination Revisited,' *Science & Justice*, vol.41 no.1 (January 2001), pp.21–32. For the case against, see R. Linsker, R.L. Garwin, H. Chernoff, P. Horowitz, and N.F. Ramsey, 'Synchronization of the Acoustic Evidence in the Assassination of President Kennedy,' *Science & Justice*, vol.45 no.4 (October 2005), pp.207–226. For a detailed account, see Donald B. Thomas, *Hear No Evil: Social Constructivism and the Forensic Evidence in the Kennedy Assassination*, Mary Ferrell Foundation Press, 2010, pp.559–690; Thomas found acoustical evidence for five shots. For a readable overview, see G. Paul Chambers, *Head Shot: The Science Behind the JFK Assassination*, Prometheus Books, 2010, pp.116–144.

3 The Case Against Oswald

Although the bullet shells and the rifle implicated Lee Oswald in the assassination, a substantial proportion of the general public either remained unconvinced that he had acted alone, or doubted that he had been involved at all. In order to help the media to "convince the public that Oswald is the real assassin,"[1] the Warren Commission was obliged to describe in detail how Oswald, without assistance, was able to kill one man and injure two others.

The Commission's case involved three essential claims: that all of the shooting came from the easternmost south–facing window on the sixth floor of the Texas School Book Depository; that Lee Harvey Oswald had brought the rifle to work, and was at the sixth floor window with the rifle at the time of the shooting; and that it was physically possible for a lone gunman to have caused all the known injuries with only three shots.

As well as the presence of the rifle and the empty bullet shells, there was other strong evidence that at least some of the shooting had come from the TSBD. Many eye–witnesses heard one or more shots from the building. Geneva Hine, for example, was watching the motorcade from her office on the second floor: "[the shots] came from inside the building ... the building vibrated from the result of the explosion." Patricia Lawrence was standing outside the TSBD: "I thought the shots had come from right over my head." Four witnesses in Dealey Plaza saw a gunman on one of the upper floors. Howard Brennan "looked up at the building. I then saw this man I have described in the window and he was taking aim with a

1. The essential purpose of what became the Warren Commission, in the words of J. Edgar Hoover: *HSCA Appendix*, vol.3, p.472.

high powered rifle. I could see all of the barrel of the gun." Arnold Rowland "saw what I thought was a man standing back about 15 feet from the windows and was holding in his arms what appeared to be a hi powered rifle because it looked as though it had a scope on it." Carolyn Walther "looked back toward the TSBD Building and saw a man . . . [who] was holding a rifle with the barrel pointed downward." Amos Euins "looked up in the red brick building. I saw a man in a window with a gun and I saw him shoot twice. He then stepped back behind some boxes. I could tell the gun was a rifle and it sounded like an automatic rifle the way he was shooting. I just saw a little bit of the barrel, and some of the trigger housing."[2]

The idea that every gunshot originated from the building's southeasternmost sixth-floor window was, however, merely the Warren Commission's working assumption. The idea had no explicit evidence in its favour, and was contradicted by several types of evidence, including the forty or so witnesses who thought that gunfire came from in front of the motorcade. Among them were two Secret Service agents. Paul Landis, who was in the car immediately behind Kennedy's, wrote that "the [fatal] shot came from somewhere towards the front." Forrest Sorrels, in the car just ahead of Kennedy's, "looked towards the top of the terrace to my right as the sound of the shots seemed to come from that direction."[3]

The location of President Kennedy's head injuries suggests that at least one shot came from somewhere other than the sixth floor. The autopsy pathologists consistently claimed that there was an entry wound low down on the back of President Kennedy's skull. There was also a large wound, the location of which was variously described as toward the top, right and rear of the skull. All of these locations of the supposed exit wound are higher than the entry wound, and are incompatible with a shot coming from above and behind at an angle of about 15 degrees to the horizontal, given the inclination of Kennedy's head at the moment of the fatal shot

2. Geneva Hine: *WCHE*, vol.6, p.395. Patricia Lawrence: CE 1381 (*WCHE*, vol.22, p.660). Howard Brennan: *WCHE*, vol.19, p.470. Arnold Rowland: CE 357 (*WCHE*, vol.16, p.953). Carolyn Walther: CE 2086 (*WCHE*, vol.24, p.522). Amos Euins: CE 367 (*WCHE*, vol.16, p.963).

3. Paul Landis: CE 1024 (*WCHE*, vol.18, p.759). Forrest Sorrels: *WCHE*, vol.21, p.548. For other examples, see Appendix C, Grassy Knoll Witnesses, p.127 below.

or shots, which is shown on frames 312 and 313 of the Zapruder film. The Warren Commission's interpretation of the head wounds is shown in CE 388, a drawing in which the angle of the head at the instant of the fatal shot does not correspond to that shown in the Zapruder film. The Clark Panel in 1968, followed by the House Select Committee on Assassinations in 1977–78, felt obliged to move the entry wound four inches or ten centimetres higher, so that it might plausibly appear to be in line with the sixth–floor window and the larger wound. Dr James Humes, the pathologist in charge of President Kennedy's autopsy, gave his opinion of the revised entry wound when it was indicated to him on a photograph of Kennedy's head: "I can assure you that as we reflected the scalp to get to this point, there was no defect corresponding to this in the skull at any point. I don't know what that is. It could be to me clotted blood. I don't, I just don't know what it is, but it certainly was not any wound of entrance."[4]

The size of the large head wound, and the presence within the skull of dozens of tiny particles of metal, suggest that the majority of the damage to the head was caused by a soft–nosed bullet, a type designed to break apart on impact. All the non–fatal wounds to Kennedy and Connally were caused by one or more metal–jacketed bullets, which were designed to remain intact. The shells found on the sixth floor of the TSBD were all from the same batch, and must have contained the same type of bullet. The implication is that either the soft–nosed bullet was fired from elsewhere, or it was fired from the sixth floor by a second gunman, a conclusion equally unhelpful to the notion of Oswald as the lone assassin.[5]

4. CE 388: *WCHE*, vol.16, p.984. The FBI calculated the angle of a shot from the sixth floor to be between 17° and 18° a few seconds before the instant of the head shot, at which point the angle would have become slightly less acute: *WR*, p.106. Dr Humes: *HSCA Appendix*, vol.7, p.254. Individual frames of the Zapruder film can be found at http://www.assassinationresearch.com/zfilm/. For more about the medical aspects of the case, see Appendix A, The Medical Evidence, p.105 below.
5. For the ballistics aspects of the case, see: Donald B. Thomas, *Hear No Evil: Social Constructivism and the Forensic Evidence in the Kennedy Assassination*, Mary Ferrell Foundation Press, 2010, pp.297–450; G. Paul Chambers, *Head Shot: The Science Behind the JFK Assassination*, Prometheus Books, 2010, pp.195–221; and Bonar Menninger, *Mortal Error: The Shot That Killed JFK*, St. Martin's Press, 1992, pp.238–255. Menninger's treatment of the ballistics evidence is credible, although his main conclusion, that the fatal shot was fired accidentally by a Secret Service agent, is contradicted by Charles Bronson's home movie; see p.85 below.

Perhaps the best–known evidence of shooting from somewhere other than the TSBD is the motion of President Kennedy's head in reaction to the fatal shot. The sharp back–and–to–the–left movement became widely known when bootleg copies of the Zapruder film began to circulate a few years after the assassination.[6]

Other objections were made to the Commission's claim that Oswald had brought a rifle to work on the day of the assassination, that he had been on the sixth floor at the time of the shooting, and that he had fired the rifle from the sixth floor.

Only three witnesses had seen Oswald prior to and during his arrival at work on 22 November 1963. All three testified that he had not carried a rifle. Buell Wesley Frazier, who had driven Oswald to work, and his sister, Linnie Mae Randle, at whose house Oswald had met Frazier that morning, both claimed that Oswald had been carrying a paper bag, but that the bag was much too short to have held the Mannlicher Carcano rifle that was discovered on the sixth floor of the TSBD. Jack Dougherty, a colleague of Oswald's who saw him enter the TSBD, was adamant that he did not see anything in Oswald's hands. In interviews with the FBI, Randle and Frazier both claimed that the bag they saw was 27 inches (69 cm) long. The rifle, however, was 34.8 inches (88 cm) long when disassembled and 40.2 inches (102 cm) long when intact.[7] Oswald said that he had

6. The phrase "back and to the left" was popularised by Oliver Stone's film, *JFK*, and later by the TV show, *Seinfeld*, and the comedian, Bill Hicks. A Nobel Prize–winning physicist, Luis Alvarez, attempted to demonstrate that the motion was not in fact inconsistent with a shot from the sixth–floor window, which was almost directly behind the president; see Luis A. Alvarez, 'A Physicist Examines the Kennedy Assassination Film', *American Journal of Physics*, vol.44 no.9 (September 1976), pp.813–27, reproduced at *HSCA Appendix*, vol.1, pp.428–441. Against Alvarez, see e.g. Chambers, *op. cit.*, pp.163–170. It was pointed out that Alvarez's experimental method, which involved shooting at melons on a fence post, hardly resembled the conditions it was supposed to replicate. Against other aspects of Alvarez's analysis, see Michael A. Stroscio, 'More Physical Insight into the Assassination of President Kennedy', *Physics and Society*, vol.25 no.4 (October 1996), pp.7–8. Alvarez's motivation and objectivity came under suspicion when it was later revealed that his research in this area had been funded by the US government, and that in 1949 he had testified against the dissident physicist Robert Oppenheimer to the House Un-American Activities Committee. For more information, see the sources mentioned in Appendix A, The Medical Evidence, p.105 below.

7. Frazier's testimony: *WCHE*, vol.2, pp.239–43; his FBI interview: CE 2009 (*WCHE*, vol.24, p.409). Randle's testimony: *WCHE*, vol.2, pp.248–50; her FBI interview: CE 2009 (*WCHE*, vol.24, p.408). Dougherty's testimony: *WCHE*, vol.6, pp.376–377. The length of the rifle: *WCHE*, vol.3, p.395.

brought a sandwich and an apple to work, a claim corroborated by his wife, so Dougherty must have been mistaken about having seen nothing in Oswald's hands.[8] Overlooking a small lunch bag is perhaps understandable; overlooking a bag containing a long rifle, on the other hand, is not. The Warren Commission overcame the problem by claiming that all three witnesses were mistaken, which would have been a reasonable assumption had it been supported by strong independent evidence of Oswald's guilt.[9] Because the rifle can only have been stored at the house in which Oswald's family was living, and because Oswald only stayed there the night before the assassination, the only date on which Oswald plausibly could have brought the rifle to work was the day of the assassination. If, as the evidence strongly suggests, he did not do so, either Oswald had an accomplice or the rifle was taken into the building without his knowledge.

The Dallas police claimed to have discovered on the sixth floor a paper bag that was long enough to have contained the rifle. The police's fingerprint officers dusted the bag for prints; Carl Day found "no legible prints," and Robert Studebaker found "just smudges." The bag was later examined by the FBI's Sebastian Latona, who discovered a partial right palmprint and a partial left index fingerprint that could be matched to Oswald.[10]

Although the bag, or at least the paper that was used to make the bag, had come into contact with Oswald's hands at some point, it may not have done so while it contained the sixth–floor rifle. Frazier and Randle each claimed that the bag they were shown was substantially longer than the one they had seen, and that Oswald had carried the bag by cupping and gripping the ends of it in his right hand, a manner inconsistent with the location of the two faint prints. Nor did the bag show creases or oil stains consistent with it having held the disassembled rifle. James Cadigan, of the FBI laboratory, testified that "I was also requested ... to examine the bag to determine if there were any significant markings or scratches or

8. Oswald's lunch: *WR*, p.622. Marina Oswald: *WCHE*, vol.1, p.73.

9. "The Commission ... has concluded that Frazier and Randle are mistaken as to the length of the bag": *WR*, p.134.

10. Carl Day: *WCHE*, vol.4, p.267. Robert Studebaker: *WCHE*, vol.7, p.144. Sebastian Latona: *WCHE*, vol.4, pp.6–9. Photograph of the right palmprint: CE 632 (*WCHE*, vol.17, p.286). Photograph of the left fingerprint: CE 633 (*WCHE*, vol.17, p.287).

abrasions or anything by which it could be associated with the rifle, Commission Exhibit 139, that is, could I find any markings that I could tie to that rifle.... And I couldn't find any such markings."[11]

There are good reasons to be sceptical of the claim that the bag that was produced in evidence was found at the scene of the crime. The police officers who first came across the alleged sniper's nest gave confused testimony about whether there was a paper bag nearby, and none of the crime scene photographs showed the bag *in situ*. Roger Craig and Gerald Hill denied seeing a bag. Richard M. Sims saw what he described as "some wrappings," "a brown wrapping," "some loose paper" and "a wrapper." Marvin Johnson did see a paper bag: "L.D. Montgomery, my partner, picked it up off the floor, and it was folded up, and he unfolded it.... It was folded and then refolded. It was a fairly small package.... The sack was folded up here and it was east of the pipes in the corner. To the best of my memory, that is where my partner picked it up. I was standing there when he picked it up." Montgomery also saw a bag but denied picking it up. J.B. Hicks, of the Dallas police crime laboratory, did not recall a paper bag among the items of evidence taken from the TSBD.[12] The nearest thing to a photograph of the paper bag at the crime scene was CE 1302, a photograph showing the sniper's nest with a printed outline of the supposed location of the bag. The earliest known photographs of the bag were taken on the front steps of the TSBD shortly before 4pm, perhaps as much as three hours after the police had entered the building.[13]

It is highly unlikely that Oswald could have assembled the bag. Although the bag had been constructed from wrapping paper and tape used at the depository, it could only have been assembled at the building's wrapping table, to which Oswald did not have access. The paper and the tape both contained markings from one

11. James Cadigan: *WCHE*, vol.4, p.97. CE 139: *WCHE*, vol.16, p.512.

12. Roger Craig: *WCHE*, vol.6, p.268. Gerald Hill: *WCHE*, vol.7, p.46. Richard M. Sims: *WCHE*, vol.7, p.161. Marvin Johnson: *WCHE*, vol.7, pp.103–104. L.D. Montgomery: *WCHE*, vol.7, p.98. J.B. Hicks: *WCHE*, vol.7, p.289.

13. CE 1302: *WCHE*, vol.22, p.479. For a photograph of the bag by William Allen of the *Dallas Times Herald*, see Richard Trask, *Pictures of the Pain: Photography and the Assassination of President Kennedy*, Yeoman Press, 1994, p.552. The bag was brought out between about 2:30pm, when three tramps were photographed in Dealey Plaza, and "four o'clock ... probably later," when the photographers were let into the TSBD: *WCHE*, vol.13, p.105.

particular tape dispensing machine at the TSBD. The machine was too sturdy to have been removed from the premises, and was under constant supervision. Troy West testified that he spent his entire working day at the wrapping table, and implied that Oswald never had a chance to manufacture the bag. James Cadigan of the FBI laboratory testified that the paper and tape of the bag possessed "identical" physical characteristics to samples of wrapping paper and tape taken by the Dallas police on the afternoon of 22 November. The TSBD used approximately one roll of paper every three working days, and for each consignment of 58 rolls of paper, the company ordered a consignment of 500 rolls of tape, the equivalent of using one roll of tape roughly every three working hours, which suggests that the paper bag supposedly found on the sixth floor was constructed after Oswald's arrival at the TSBD that morning and within a short time of the samples being taken by the police.[14]

The first sighting of Oswald after the shooting was by two witnesses, a policeman and the building supervisor, who encountered him in the lunch room on the second floor of the TSBD a little more than one minute after they heard gunshots. The timing of the incident alone casts serious doubt on the claim that Oswald had been on the sixth floor during the assassination. The Commission re-enacted the movements of the two witnesses, who had come up from the first floor, and of Oswald, who in theory had come down from the sixth floor after laboriously hiding the rifle. The re-enactments were only able to get Oswald to the second floor in time to meet the witnesses by artificially quickening his descent and slowing their ascent.[15]

14. The markings on the paper: *WCHE*, vol.4, pp.90–93. Troy West: *WCHE*, vol.6, pp.360–362. James Cadigan: *WCHE*, vol.4, p.93. The TSBD's use of paper: *WCHE*, vol.4, p.96. Its use of tape: CD 897, p.163. For detailed accounts of the paper bag, see Ian Griggs, 'The Paper Bag that Never Was, part 1,' *Dealey Plaza Echo*, vol.1, no.1, July 1996, pp.30–36; Ian Griggs, 'The Paper Bag that Never Was, part 2,' *Dealey Plaza Echo*, vol.1, no.2, November 1996, pp.30–38; and Sylvia Meagher, *Accessories After the Fact: the Warren Commission, the Authorities, and the Report*, Vintage, 1992, pp.45–64.

15. The Warren Commission's account of Oswald's descent to the second floor: *WR*, pp.149–153. For the problems with this account, see David Wrone, *The Zapruder Film: Reframing JFK's Assassination*, University Press of Kansas, 2003, pp.170–171, and Howard Roffman, *Presumed Guilty: How and Why the Warren Commission Framed Lee Harvey Oswald*, Fairleigh Dickinson University Press, 1975, pp.108–112.

The Commission brushed aside evidence from other people within the TSBD who would have seen or heard anyone dashing down the stairs, but who failed to do so. On each floor, the enclosed wooden staircase opened onto a landing, which anyone using the stairs was obliged to cross. Several employees were on or close to the stairs and could be expected to have seen or heard Oswald on his journey to the second floor, but none did. Jack Dougherty was working on the fifth floor close to the stairs; he heard a shot from the floor above him, but did not report any sound or movement from the stairs. Nor did he or the other three workers on the fifth floor hear anyone shifting cartons of books, which would have been necessary in order to hide the rifle. Victoria Adams and Sandra Styles were with two colleagues on the fourth floor at the time of the shooting. Adams and Styles immediately ran to the stairway. Adams was asked specifically if she had seen or heard anyone else on the stairs, and replied that she had not. Styles and her other two colleagues were not questioned. One of the other two colleagues did, however, make a signed statement in which she claimed that she saw Adams and Styles descend and the policeman and supervisor ascend, and that she did not see Oswald. The known facts of the encounter with the policeman and the supervisor are entirely consistent with Oswald having ascended from the first floor by a more direct route than that taken by the witnesses.[16]

Descriptions of the gunman's physical features and clothing are contradictory and inconclusive. Four people are known to have seen a man with a rifle on the sixth floor of the TSBD, but only one of them, Howard Brennan, provided a detailed identification that came close to matching Oswald's appearance. In a statement on the day of the assassination, Brennan claimed that the gunman was "a white man in his early 30's, slender, nice looking, slender and would weigh about 165 to 175 pounds." In his Warren Commission testimony, Brennan gave the man's height as five feet ten

16. Jack Dougherty: *WCHE*, vol.6, pp.380–381. The other three workers on the fifth floor were Bonnie Ray Williams (*WCHE*, vol.3, pp.161–184), Harold Norman (*WCHE*, vol.3, pp.186–198), and James Jarman (*WCHE*, vol.3, pp.198–211). Victoria Adams: *WCHE*, vol.6, pp.388–390. For the statement by Dorothy Garner, see Barry Ernest, *The Girl on the Stairs: My Search for a Missing Witness to the Assassination of John F. Kennedy*, Createspace, 2011.

inches. Arnold Rowland, who also saw a gunman, and Ronald Fischer, who did not notice a gun, both described the man they saw as "slender," and Fischer added that "he looked to be 22 or 24 years old." Lee Harvey Oswald was white, slender, and 24 years old. Official documents give his adult height as either five feet nine inches (175 cm) or five feet ten inches. On the day of his arrest, he weighed 131 pounds (59 kg). All three descriptions could reasonably have applied to Oswald, but could also have applied to any number of young white men.[17]

Brennan, however, turned out to be unreliable and unhelpful. He claimed that the gunman had been standing up when firing, although the half–open window required any gunman to have crouched or kneeled. He claimed to have seen the gunman's trousers, which would not have been visible from Brennan's viewpoint on the street 60 feet or 18 metres below. When asked whether he had actually seen the firing of the rifle, he replied, "No." He claimed that on hearing the first shot, "I looked up at the building. I then saw this man I have described in the window and he was taking aim with a high powered rifle. I could see all of the barrel of the gun." Brennan's reaction to the first shot is visible on the Zapruder film: standing directly opposite the sixth–floor window, he watches Kennedy's car go past him to his left, then from about frame 204 he in fact turns his head sharply to his right, away from the TSBD, rather than up toward the sixth floor. He attended a line–up on the day of the assassination, but "said he was unable to make a positive identification," despite already having seen Oswald's picture on television. A few weeks later, his memory improved and he informed the FBI that he could identify Oswald. The next month, he changed his mind again and "appeared to revert to his earlier inability to make a positive identification." In the absence of any other plausible candidates, the Commission nominated Brennan as the source of the Dallas police radio despatcher's description of the gunman, but his limited credibility as a witness

17. Howard Brennan's testimony: *WCHE*, vol.3, pp.142–158. His statement to the Dallas Sheriff's office on the afternoon of the assassination, in which he describes the gunman: *WCHE*, vol.19, p.470. Arnold Rowland: CE 358 (*WCHE*, vol.16, p.954) and *WCHE*, vol.2, p.169. Ronald Fischer: *WCHE*, vol.6, p.194. For Oswald's height, see his autopsy report: CE 3002 (*WCHE*, vol.26, p.521). For Oswald's weight, see his arrest form: CE 630 (*WCHE*, vol.17, p.285).

raises uncomfortable questions about the actual source. The House Select Committee on Assassinations declined to use Howard Brennan's testimony.[18]

Arnold Rowland claimed that the gunman had "dark hair ... it was dark, probably black." Amos Euins stated that "I seen a bald spot on this man's head, trying to look out the window. He had a bald spot on his head. I was looking at the bald spot." Oswald's hair was light brown; it was receding slightly at the temples, but he did not have a bald spot. Two other witnesses, however, described the colour of the man's hair in a way that did apply to Oswald: Robert Edwards claimed that it was "light brown," and Carolyn Walther remembered "blond or light brown hair."[19]

Five of the six witnesses who saw a man on the sixth floor of the TSBD were able to describe his clothing. All five said that he was wearing light–coloured clothes. Howard Brennan: "He had on light colored clothing"; "Light colored clothes, more of a khaki color." Arnold Rowland: "He had on a light shirt, a very light–colored shirt, white or a light blue or a color such as that. This was open at the collar. I think it was unbuttoned about halfway, and then he had a regular T–shirt, a polo shirt under this." Carolyn Walther: "a white shirt." Ronald Fischer: the shirt was "light in color; probably white ... it was open–neck and light in color." Robert Edwards: "light colored shirt, short sleeve and open neck."[20] Oswald did not wear a light–coloured shirt with an open neck on the day of the assassination. At the time of his arrest, he was wearing a brown shirt over a white T–shirt, and dark trousers. Oswald claimed to have changed out of a "reddish colored, long sleeved, shirt with a button–down collar" between the assassination and his arrest. He had certainly been wearing a dark shirt that morning; Linnie Mae Randle stated that "I remember some sort of brown or tan shirt." Marrion Baker, the policeman who encountered Oswald on the second floor immediately after the shooting, said that Oswald was wearing "a brown–type shirt" that was per-

18. Brennan: *WCHE*, vol.3, p.143. "Unable to make a positive identification": *WR*, p.145. Attribution of police description to Brennan: *WR*, p.144.
19. Arnold Rowland: *WCHE*, vol.2, p.171. Amos Euins: *WCHE*, vol.2, p.204. Robert Edwards: *WCHE*, vol.6, p.203. Carolyn Walther: CE 2086 (*WCHE*, vol.24, p.522).
20. Howard Brennan: *WCHE*, vol.3, p.145. Arnold Rowland: *WCHE*, vol.2, p.171. Carolyn Walther: CE 2086 (*WCHE*, vol.24, p.522). Ronald Fischer: *WCHE*, vol.6, p.194. Robert Edwards: *WCHE*, vol.6, p.203.

haps "a little bit darker" than the one the suspect wore after his arrest. Jeraldean Reid, on the other hand, who saw Oswald shortly after his encounter with Baker, claimed that he was wearing "a white T shirt" with no shirt or jacket.[21] Howard Brennan pointed out that Oswald at the police station "was not dressed in the same clothes that I saw the man in the window ... he just didn't have the same clothes on." The Commission reacted to Brennan's unexpected information by abruptly dismissing him:

Mr Brennan : ... he just didn't have the same clothes on.

Mr Belin : All right.

Mr Brennan : I don't know whether you have that in the record or not. I am sure you do.

Mr Dulles : Any further questions? I guess there are no more questions, Mr Belin.

Mr Belin : Well, sir, we want to thank you for your cooperation with the Commission.[22]

The Warren Commission recognised that if Oswald were the lone assassin, he must have been on the sixth floor for some time before the assassination, assembling his rifle and his sniper's nest. The Commission supported its case that Oswald had been hiding on the sixth floor by claiming that "Charles Givens ... was the last known employee to see Oswald inside the building prior to the assassination," on the sixth floor shortly after 11:45am.[23] Givens' testimony may not be reliable, however. It contradicts a statement he had made to the FBI on the day after the assassination, in which he claimed that his sighting of Oswald at 11:50 occurred on the first floor "in the domino room where the employees eat lunch." A few weeks before Givens testified before the Warren Commission, an FBI memo had pointed out that a Dallas police inspector "stated that GIVENS had been previously handled by the Special Services

21. Oswald's shirt: *WR*, p.622; see also Handwritten notes of Captain J.W. Fritz's interview of Oswald, p.7. Linnie Mae Randle: *WCHE*, vol.2, p.250. Marrion Baker: *WCHE*, vol.3, p.257. Jeraldean Reid, whose first name is given elsewhere as Geraldean, and who is referred to here as Mrs Robert Reid: *WCHE*, vol.3, p.276.
22. Howard Brennan: *WCHE*, vol.3, p.161.
23. *WR*, p.143.

Bureau on a marijuana charge and he believes that GIVENS would change his story for money."[24]

If Oswald had indeed been on the sixth floor shortly before mid–day, he did not stay long. A colleague of his, Bonnie Ray Williams, spent about 10 minutes on the sixth floor from around 12:00, and claimed that he was the only person present on that floor.[25] It is quite possible that Oswald had not set foot on the sixth floor for an hour or more before the assassination. Although he had visited the sixth floor that morning, he had been working on the fifth floor immediately before beginning his lunch break at about 11:45.[26]

Charles Givens was not in fact "the last known employee to see Oswald inside the building prior to the assassination." Three other employees saw Oswald on either the first or second floor during the thirty minutes or so immediately before the assassination. Two of Oswald's colleagues, William Shelley and Eddie Piper, corroborated Givens' original statement, testifying that Oswald had been on the first floor at around mid–day.[27] Another TSBD employee, Carolyn Arnold, stated in interviews with the FBI that she saw Oswald on either the first or second floor at either 12:15 or 12:25.[28] She clarified the time and place in later interviews: "she saw Oswald in the 2nd–floor lunchroom as she was on her way out of the depository to watch the presidential motorcade.... She left the building at 12:25pm."[29] "About a quarter of an hour before the assassination, I went into the lunchroom on the second floor," where she saw Oswald.[30] At the same time as Oswald was seen on the second floor, however, a gunman was already in place on the sixth floor. Arnold Rowland, standing outside the building, told the FBI that "Between 12:10 p.m. and 12:15 p.m., ... I observed the two rect-

24. Charles Givens' testimony, on 8 April 1964: *WCHE*, vol.6, p.352. His original statement, dated 23 November 1963: CD 5, p.329. The FBI memo, dated 13 February 1964: CD 735, p.295. For a detailed discussion of this unsavoury episode, see Sylvia Meagher, 'The Curious Testimony of Mr Givens,' *Texas Observer*, 13 August 1971.
25. Bonnie Ray Williams: *WCHE*, vol.3, pp.169–170.
26. Oswald on the fifth floor: *WCHE*, vol.3, p.168.
27. William Shelley: *WCHE*, vol.6, p.328. Eddie Piper: *WCHE*, vol.19, p.499.
28. Carolyn Arnold: CD 5, p.41; CD 706, p.7.
29. Earl Golz, 'Was Oswald in Window?,' *Dallas Morning News*, 26 November 1978, p.13A.
30. Anthony Summers, *Not in Your Lifetime: The Assassination of JFK*, Headline, 2013, p.92.

angular windows at the extreme west end of the Texas School Book Depository next to the top floor were open. I saw what I believed to be a man standing about 12 to 15 feet back from the window on the right. He ... appeared to [be] holding a rifle with scope attached, in a ready position or in military terminology, port arms."[31] The Commission ignored Carolyn Arnold's FBI statements; it did not call her to testify; it did not call any of her colleagues who could have corroborated or refuted her account; and it claimed on spurious grounds that Rowland was unreliable. Dismissing the evidence of Arnold Rowland served another purpose. He was one of two witnesses who saw the gunman standing next to another man on the sixth floor. The second witness, Carolyn Walther, was not called to give testimony.[32]

It is curious that none of the suriviving documents contains an account by the accused assassin of his precise location at the precise time of the shooting. During the two days between his arrest and his murder while in police custody, Oswald was questioned for a total of about twelve hours by officials from the Dallas police, the FBI, the Secret Service and even the Post Office. Some, but not all, of those who questioned Oswald later put down their memories on paper. The existing notes and memos cover only a small part of Oswald's questioning.[33]

In 1963, the Dallas Police Department was not in the habit of using a tape recorder when questioning suspects,[34] a policy unlikely to have been motivated purely by budgetary constraints. In recent years, DNA analysis has brought to light a spate of wrongful convictions in Dallas County. Most of them were perpetrated by the regime that was in office at the time of the JFK assassination, as a *Dallas Morning News* article points out: "Police officers used suggestive lineup procedures, sometimes pressured victims to pick their suspect and then cleared the case once an identification was made.... All but five of the wrongful convictions occurred under

31. Arnold Rowland: CE 358 (*WCHE*, vol.16, p.954). Rowland repeated his claim to the Warren Commission: *WCHE*, vol.2, p.169.

32. Rowland saw a second man: *WCHE*, vol.2, pp.174–175. Carolyn Walther: CE 2086 (*WCHE*, vol.24, p.522).

33. Records of Oswald's interrogation: *WR*, pp.598–636.

34. The Dallas police were not alone in this; see Thomas P. Sullivan, 'Police Experiences with Recording Custodial Interrogations,' *Judicature*, vol.88 no.3 (November–December 2004), pp.132–136.

the late District Attorney Henry Wade."[35] Improper police procedures were certainly used against Oswald. In particular, at least one witness was required to sign a statement identifying Oswald before he had attended a line–up.[36] Neither the gravity of the crime nor the attention of the world's press appear to have provided the Dallas police with sufficient motivation to change their policy of not recording interviews. Several shorthand secretaries worked in the Dallas police headquarters, but none seems to have been called upon to transcribe the defendant's replies to his questioning. It is unlikely that any recordings or transcripts were made of Oswald's twelve hours of interrogation.

According to a report by FBI agents who interviewed the suspect, "OSWALD claimed to be on the first floor when President JOHN F. KENNEDY passed this building."[37] The most detailed account of Oswald's alibi is in a report by Captain J.W. Fritz of the Dallas police: "I asked him what part of the building he was in at the time the president was shot, and he said that he was having his lunch about that time on the first floor."[38] It is inconceivable that even the Dallas police would have been satisfied with an account of what their only suspect was doing at "about" the time of the assassination. Because no mention is made of Oswald refusing to provide a precise alibi, one might reasonably suspect that a precise alibi was given, and that it contained information that could have been, and perhaps was, checked for corroboration.

Oswald does have an alibi for the few minutes before the assassination. An FBI agent who interviewed him wrote that "Oswald stated that ... he had eaten lunch in the lunch room at the Texas School Book Depository, alone, but recalled possibly two Negro employees walking through the room during this period. He stated possibly one of these employees was called 'Junior' and the other

35. Steve McGonigle and Jennifer Emily, '18 Dallas County Cases Overturned by DNA Relied Heavily on Eyewitness Testimony,' *Dallas Morning News*, 12 October 2008.

36. William Whaley: *WCHE*, vol.6, p.430. The detective involved, James Leavelle, implied that the same procedure was used with two other witnesses: *WCHE*, vol.7, p.264. For an example of "suggestive lineup procedures," see *WCHE*, vol.2, pp.260–261.

37. FBI agents James Hosty and James Bookhout: *WR*, p.613. For speculation about which part of the first floor Oswald was on, see Appendix E, Was Oswald Standing in the Doorway?, p.169 below.

38. Captain Fritz: *WR*, p.600.

was a short individual."[39] The notes of Captain Fritz corroborate this: "say[s] two negr came in. One Jr. + short negro."[40] Two black employees matched these descriptions: James Jarman was known as 'Junior', and Harold Norman was short.

Both men had been standing outside the TSBD, waiting to see the president. When they heard that the motorcade had reached Main Street, they decided to go back into the building to obtain a better view. Because of the crowd standing on the front steps of the TSBD, they used one of the building's rear entrances. Their route around the north–east corner of the building took them right past the windows of the first–floor lunch room, known as the domino room, the location where Charles Givens originally stated that he had seen Oswald reading a newspaper shortly before mid–day. They would have entered the building very close to the door of the domino room. Oswald could hardly have known about their presence in this part of the TSBD unless he too had been on the first floor at the time. According to police logs, the motorcade was on Main Street from about 12:23pm until 12:29pm, which places Oswald on the first floor just a few minutes before the shooting. Jarman narrows the time further: he was standing outside "until about 12:20, between 12:20 and 12:25."[41] A second–hand version of Oswald's alibi has him claiming to have eaten lunch with 'Junior' Jarman, which Jarman denied. This denial allowed the *Warren Report* to dismiss without argument Oswald's claim that he was on the first floor five or ten minutes before the assassination, at a time when an assassin would surely have been in place on the sixth floor.[42]

There are many reasons to doubt that all the shots had been fired from the sixth floor of the TSBD, that Lee Harvey Oswald

39. Bookhout: *WR*, p.622.
40. Fritz: Handwritten notes of Captain J.W. Fritz's interview of Oswald, p.1.
41. The Dallas Police radio log states that at 12:22pm the motorcade was on Harwood Street and "just about to cross Live Oak [Street]" (*WCHE*, vol.17, p.461). Main Street was about one minute further on. James Jarman: *WCHE*, vol.3, pp.201–202. Harold Norman: *WCHE*, vol.3, pp.189–190. For a plan of the first (i.e. ground) floor, see *WR*, p.148 (CE 1061). A more detailed plan is available at Baylor University, Poage Library, Robert Cutler Collection; online at http://digitalcollections.baylor.edu/cdm/ref/collection/po-jfkgkgaz/id/1263. The domino room was in the north–east corner, overlooking the loading bay. CD 81 and CD 496 contain photographs of the domino room.
42. *WR*, p.182.

had brought a rifle into the building, and that Oswald had been on the sixth floor during the shooting. The final, and perhaps the most important, element of the case against Oswald required the three bullet shells to be matched to the wounds. Several facts soon emerged which greatly constrained any explanation of how a lone gunman, in the time available, could fire one particular rifle from one particular location and cause one particular set of wounds.

The first constraint is that if Oswald's rifle fired all the shots, there must have been a minimum of 2.3 seconds between each shot. The rifle discovered on the sixth floor was examined and tested by the US Army and the FBI, who found that it was in a much poorer condition than most rifles of its type. It could not be aimed accurately, and so it was tested mainly for the speed with which it could fire a sequence of shots. In a series of tests by skilled marksmen, the fastest time taken to operate the bolt and the trigger pull, without aiming the rifle, was 2.3 seconds. A gunman firing that particular rifle at a moving target from 60 feet above, and scoring two hits out of three, would need to be particularly skillful to take just 2.3 seconds per shot. The army's experts, having adjusted the sixth–floor rifle to improve its accuracy, fired seven groups of three shots at stationary targets from 30 feet above. Their times were: 4.45, 4.6, 5.15, 6.45, 6.75, 7, and 8.25 seconds. Of the 21 shots, 20 missed the heads and shoulders of the silhouettes on the targets.[43]

The second constraint is that if Oswald's rifle were the only weapon used, all the injuries had to have been caused by no more than three bullets. Three empty rifle bullet shells were found on the sixth floor of the Texas School Book Depository, all of them close to the window in the south–eastern corner. One unfired bullet was found in the rifle. No other rifle bullets or bullet shells were discovered in the building, or on Oswald's person, or among his belongings.

The third constraint is that if every shot was fired by Oswald from the easternmost sixth–floor window, all the shooting must have taken place within six seconds. Abraham Zapruder's famous home movie of the shooting allowed the timing of Kennedy's progress along the road to be accurately determined. As Kennedy's

43. "At least 2.3 seconds were required between shots": *WR*, p.97. The army's test times: *WCHE*, vol.3, p.446. The FBI's test times: *WCHE*, vol.3, pp.403–410.

car passed the TSBD, it was hidden at first from the sixth–floor window by an oak tree. There was a period of just under six seconds between the car becoming visible to anyone in the easternmost sixth–floor window, which occurred at frame 210 of the Zapruder film, and the moment of the fatal head shot, which occurred immediately after frame 312. At 18.3 frames per second, Zapruder's camera took 103 frames in just under six seconds. The *Warren Report* pointed out that the time might increase to eight seconds or more if either the first or the final shot had missed, but the Commission recognised that this was highly unlikely: the first shot could not plausibly have been fired from the sixth floor while President Kennedy was hidden behind the tree, and there is no reason to suppose that the final shot was not the one which hit Kennedy in the head. The sighting of Oswald by witnesses on the second floor shortly after the shooting requires him to have left the sixth floor as soon as possible after the head shot.[44]

For Oswald to have been the lone gunman, all of the following constraints had to apply: there were at least 2.3 seconds between each shot; no more than three bullets caused all of the wounds; and the whole shooting took no longer than six seconds. If any of these statements were contradicted by the balance of the evidence, Oswald could not have committed the crime alone. The Warren Commission attempted to deal with these constraints by devising what became known as the single–bullet theory.

44. The time available for all the shots: *WR*, p.117.

4 The Single–Bullet Theory

The first official report into the assassination, the *FBI Summary Report* of December 1963, devoted only a few words to a description of the wounds: "two bullets struck President Kennedy, and one wounded Governor Connally," and "one of the bullets [that struck Kennedy] had entered just below his shoulder to the right of his spinal column at an angle of 45 to 60 degrees downward ... there was no point of exit." The report, which was based on the written account of the two FBI agents who attended the president's autopsy, gave no description of Connally's injuries, and entirely failed to mention Kennedy's throat wound and James Tague's wound. It appears to match the wounds to the three bullet shells in the following way: one bullet caused some or all of Governor Connally's wounds; one bullet caused President Kennedy's fatal head wound; and one bullet caused the non–fatal wound in Kennedy's back but did not cause his throat wound. The report implies that at least one more bullet was fired, making at least four in total.[1]

In March 1964, the Warren Commission modified this explanation by assuming that Kennedy's throat wound had been caused by the same bullet that had caused his back wound. An internal memo in April set down the sequence of events: "Our report presumably will show that the President was hit by the first bullet, Governor Connally by the second, and the President by the third and fatal bullet. The report will also conclude that the bullets were fired by one person located in the sixth floor southeast corner

1. *FBI Summary Report*: CD 1; see pp.1 and 18. The agents' account of the autopsy is commonly known as the Sibert and O'Neill Report: ARRB Medical Document 44.

window of the TSBD building."[2] By June 1964, when the wounding of the bystander, James Tague, had unexpectedly been made public, the Commission became obliged to use the only plausible explanation that would account for all of the wounds having been inflicted by just three bullets: one bullet caused Tague's wound; one bullet caused President Kennedy's fatal head wound; and one bullet caused all of Kennedy's and Connally's non–fatal wounds by entering Kennedy's back, exiting through his throat, entering Connally's back, exiting his chest, passing through his right wrist, and lodging itself in his left thigh.

This is the single–bullet theory. James Tague's wound demanded its own bullet because he was too far away for his injury plausibly to have been caused by a fragment of a bullet which had struck Kennedy or Connally. President Kennedy's head wound demanded its own bullet because it clearly occurred later than at least some of his and Connally's non–fatal wounds. That left a single bullet to create all the other wounds. The single–bullet theory had been proposed a few weeks earlier by Arlen Specter, one of the Commission's junior counsel, but it was the publicity attached to Tague's wounding that forced the Commission to adopt the theory.[3]

Two aspects of the evidence suggest that the single–bullet theory is plausible. Firstly, no bullets or bullet fragments were discovered in President Kennedy's body at the autopsy, apart from the many small fragments associated with his head wound.[4] Secondly, although the photographic evidence does not allow the horizontal alignment of the president and Governor Connally to be accurately determined, it does not rule out the possibility that a bullet fired from the south–eastern corner of the Texas School Book Depository might have passed through both men.

2. Norman Redlich to J. Lee Rankin, 27 April 1964, National Archives; reproduced in Barb Junkkarinen, 'First Shot / First Hit Circa Z–190,' *Kennedy Assassination Chronicles*, vol.5 no.2 (Summer 1999), p.28.

3. The *Warren Report*'s account of the single–bullet theory: *WR*, p.117. For the development of the single–bullet theory, see Gerald D. McKnight, *Breach of Trust: How the Warren Commission Failed the Nation and Why*, University Press of Kansas, 2005, pp.181–212.

4. The Clark Panel in 1968 noted that X–rays of Kennedy's neck revealed tiny fragments of metal, but this was disputed by the HSCA's medical panel; see *HSCA Appendix*, vol.1, pp.304–305.

Although objections were raised to all of the important parts of the Warren Commission's account, the most powerful objections were aimed at the most fundamental part, the idea that all of Kennedy's and Connally's non–fatal wounds were caused by one bullet. If the single–bullet theory is false, at least one shot must have been fired by someone other than Oswald. In other words, either Oswald was working with at least one accomplice or Oswald fired none of the shots himself.

One such objection came from Governor Connally. He testified to the Warren Commission that the bullet which struck him in the back was fired later than the bullet which caused at least one of President Kennedy's non–fatal wounds. Connally maintained for the rest of his life that he was struck by a separate bullet after Kennedy had already been wounded. He was quoted in the *Washington Post* on 21 November 1966, saying that "there is my absolute knowledge that . . . one bullet caused the president's first wound and that an entirely separate shot struck me. It is a certainty. I will never change my mind." It was Connally's testimony that persuaded one of the Warren Commissioners, Senator Richard Russell, that the single–bullet theory was untenable.[5]

Two of the closest eye–witnesses independently claimed that Governor Connally's back wound was caused by a separate bullet. Connally's wife, Nellie, who was sitting to his left, stated that "I turned over my right shoulder and looked back, and saw the President as he had both hands at his neck. . . . Then very soon there was the second shot that hit John." James Chaney was one of four police motorcyclists who had a close–up view of the shooting. None of the four was invited to testify before the Warren Commission. The opinion of Chaney, who was riding to President Kennedy's right, is known from the testimony of another policeman, Marrion Baker: "I talked to Jim Chaney, and he made the statement that the two shots hit Kennedy first and then the other one hit the Governor."[6]

This was consistent with the evidence provided by the Zapruder film. The film shows President Kennedy emerging from behind

5. John Connally: *WCHE*, vol.4, pp.135–136.
6. Nellie Connally: *WCHE*, vol.4, p.147. Marrion Baker: *WCHE*, vol.3, p.266. Chaney, incidentally, was filmed on the afternoon of 22 November stating to a reporter that the fatal shot had "hit him [Kennedy] in the face;" see David Wrone, *The Zapruder Film: Reframing JFK's Assassination*, University Press of Kansas, 2003, p.184.

a road sign at about frame 225, with his hands reaching to his throat. He has clearly been shot by this point. Indeed, the single–bullet theory demands that he has been shot by this point. The Warren Commission implied that Kennedy had in fact been shot two–thirds of a second earlier, at frame 210, the instant at which he became visible from the easternmost sixth–floor window after being hidden behind an oak tree. Connally, however, shows no sign of being shot in the back until two–thirds of a second later, at about frame 238, when he starts to twist and fall to his left. This bullet arrived much too late to have been the one which wounded Kennedy, and much too early for both to have been fired from the rifle attributed to Oswald.

A later theory claimed that frame 224 of the Zapruder film, which shows the right lapel of Connally's jacket flapping outward, depicts the instant at which Connally was shot. The motion of Connally's lapel cannot have been caused by the same bullet that caused President Kennedy's throat wound, for two reasons. Firstly, the bullet that passed through the front of Connally's jacket did so several inches from the lapel. Secondly, too much time had elapsed between Kennedy's throat wound and Connally's lapel flap. The minimum time for a neurological reaction to an external stimulus is 200 milliseconds, or between three and four frames of the Zapruder film. Because Kennedy's hands can be seen to be moving toward his throat in frame 224, the wound to which he is responding cannot have occurred any later than frame 221. A hypothetical bullet fired from the rifle found on the sixth floor would have travelled at least 400 feet, or 120 metres, between the time of Kennedy's throat wound and the time of Connally's lapel flap. The distance between Kennedy and Connally was about three feet, or one metre. The flapping of Connally's lapel was probably caused by nothing more sinister than a gust of wind.[7]

Another item of Connally's clothing indicated that he was shot later than Kennedy. The governor of Texas was holding a cowboy hat in his right hand. Both the hat and the hand are visible in the Zapruder film intermittently for several seconds after Kennedy comes into view while clutching at his throat. As late as frame 268,

7. For details, see G. Paul Chambers, *Head Shot: The Science Behind the JFK Assassination*, Prometheus Books, 2010, pp.155–158.

more than two seconds after frame 225, Connally's hand is gripping his hat tightly, his shirt cuff white and free of blood. Clearly, he has not yet been hit by the bullet which clipped the end of his jacket sleeve, passed through his shirt cuff, then shattered the radius bone in his wrist and severed the tendon by his thumb.[8]

The documentary record of President Kennedy's autopsy is severely and inexcusably deficient. Consequently, the locations of none of his wounds are known with any precision. The back wound, for example, was not measured against a standard anatomical feature, and was photographed with the body in a distorted position. The fundamental question, of whether or not the back and throat wounds were caused by the same bullet, could have been answered by dissecting the wounds and the connecting tissue, but the pathologists were ordered by senior military officers not to do this. Nevertheless, what is known of the location of President Kennedy's wounds strongly undermines the single–bullet theory. Because Kennedy was sitting upright until he was shot, his throat wound was far too high, or his back wound far too low, for them both to have been caused by one bullet fired from the Texas School Book Depository's sixth floor, which was 60 feet or 18 metres above the road.[9]

The throat wound was located just below the Adam's apple and just above the knot of the tie. Dr Charles Carrico, who saw Kennedy's throat wound before it was distorted during a tracheotomy and before the president's shirt and tie were removed, was asked to point to the location on his own throat. His questioner clarified the location for the record:

> **Mr Dulles** : And you put your hand right above where your tie is?
>
> **Dr Carrico** : Yes, sir.[10]

8. For the location of the damage to Governor Connally's shirt and jacket, see *WR*, p.94. For the surgeon's description of Connally's shattered wrist, see *WCHE*, vol.4, pp.118–121. For the severed tendon, see *WCHE*, vol.4, p.124. Nellie Connally later claimed that her husband was still holding onto his hat while laying across the car seat on arrival at Parkland Hospital.

9. This objection applies not only to the single–bullet theory but almost certainly to the FBI's four–shot scenario as well. For the conduct of the autopsy, and other aspects of the medical evidence, see Appendix A, The Medical Evidence, p.105 below.

10. Dr Carrico: *WCHE*, vol.3, pp.361–362.

The Warren Commission preferred to place the bullet wound about one inch lower, just below the level of Kennedy's collar button. This location is contradicted by the lack of an obvious bullet hole in the front of Kennedy's shirt, and by the absence of bullet damage to his tie. There were several slits in the president's jacket, tie and shirt, but all of them are consistent with having been made in the hospital's emergency room by nurses using scalpels or scissors to free the patient's clothing.[11] The two cuts close to the collar of the shirt do not appear to match each other, as those caused by an intact bullet would have done.[12] The cuts in the president's shirt lay directly underneath the knot of the tie, but there was no damage to the knot of the tie apart from a tiny nick on the front of the knot, to the wearer's left. Material surrounding the nick was removed in order to obtain a sample for testing, to see whether a bullet had deposited traces of copper. Although there were traces of copper around the bullet hole in the back of the shirt, there were none on the tie or on the front of the shirt.[13] The damage to the tie, just like the damage to the front of the shirt, was evidently made by a surgical instrument, not by a bullet.

It makes no practical difference whether President Kennedy's throat wound was located at or just above the knot of his tie. The balance of the evidence places his back wound several inches lower than either location. The death certificate signed by Dr George Burkley, the president's personal doctor, who was present both in the emergency room at the hospital in Dallas and at the autopsy at Bethesda Naval Hospital Center in Maryland, located the back

11. One of the nurses stated that they "cut off his clothing": *WCHE*, vol.6, p.136. CE 393 (*WCHE*, vol.17, p.23) reveals several obvious cuts in Kennedy's jacket.
12. The *Warren Report* asserted on p.92 that "these two holes fell into alinement on overlapping positions when the shirt was buttoned. Each hole was a vertical, ragged slit." The FBI's Exhibit 60 includes a photograph of the two slits in the collar, which shows that they do not line up completely: the slits are of different shapes, and the one below the button–hole extends higher than the one below the button. This exhibit was withheld from official publication, but is reproduced at: McKnight, *op. cit.*, p.241; Harold Weisberg, *Never Again*, Carroll and Graf, 1995, p.245; and Robert Groden, *The Killing of a President*, Viking Studio Press, 1993, p.77. A close–up of the slits in the collar is available online at http://www.maryferrell.org/wiki/images/a/a5/Pict_essay_mcknightsbt_shirt_lrg.jpg. The photographs of Kennedy's shirt in CE 394 (*WCHE*, vol.17, pp.25–26) are insufficiently detailed to show the cuts in the front or the bullet hole in the back.
13. The traces of copper on the back, but not the front, of Kennedy's shirt: FBI HQ JFK Assassination File, 62–109060–14.

wound "at about the level of the third thoracic vertebra," which is typically four to six inches, or 10 to 15 centimetres, below the top of the shirt collar.[14] The autopsy descriptive sheet, made by one of the pathologists during the autopsy and endorsed as correct ("Verified") by Dr Burkley, was the official diagram of the wounds to the body. It, too, placed the back wound in this location.[15] The Sibert and O'Neill Report, the only surviving contemporary report of the autopsy, supported this location. It described "a bullet hole which was below the shoulders and two inches to the right of the middle line of the spinal column."[16] In private, the Warren Commission was aware of the problem. A transcript of an early executive session includes the remark that "the bullet entered below the shoulder blade to the right of the backbone, which is below the place where the picture shows the bullet came out."[17] The Sibert and O'Neill Report went on to contradict two other essential elements of the single–bullet theory: "it was determined that the trajectory of the missile entering at this point had entered at a downward position of 45 to 60 degrees. Further probing determined that the distance travelled by this missile was a short distance inasmuch as the end of the opening could be felt with the finger."

The backs of Kennedy's jacket and shirt each contained a bullet hole located between five and six inches below the top of the collar, which matched the location given in the death certificate.[18] Although the jacket had bunched up slightly from time to time during the motorcade as Kennedy waved to the crowd, it had never bunched up sufficiently to allow a bullet to enter at the required angle. In a photograph taken no more than 1.2 seconds before any non–fatal shot from the sixth floor could have been fired, the jacket can clearly be seen to be at or very close to its normal position. Photograph no.5 by Phil Willis corresponds to frame 202 of the Za-

14. Dr Burkley's death certificate: ARRB Medical Document 6, p.2. Two other death certificates exist, but neither one mentions the location of the back wound with any precision. For the location of the third thoracic vertebra, see http://en.wikipedia.org/wiki/File:Orientation.PNG, on which the third thoracic vertebra is marked 'T3'.

15. ARRB Medical Document 1.

16. ARRB Medical Document 44, p.4.

17. Warren Commission Executive Session, 27 January 1963, p.193.

18. For the location of the holes in President Kennedy's jacket and shirt, see *WR*, p. 92 and FBI HQ JFK Assassination File, 62–109060–14. The photographs in FBI Exhibit 60 show the locations; see note 12 above.

pruder film, and is the photograph that was taken closest in time to the hypothetical shot from the sixth floor. Frame 202 occurs just under half a second before frame 210, the first point at which Kennedy would have become visible to a sixth–floor gunman, and 1.2 seconds before frame 224, the frame in which Kennedy comes into view while reacting to his throat wound. Willis himself claimed that he took the photograph in immediate response to hearing the first shot, which, if true, would by itself disprove the single–bullet theory.[19]

Buttoned–up shirts tend to be much less flexible than jackets. President Kennedy's shirt in particular is unlikely to have bunched up significantly: it had been made to measure; it was held in place by a belt; it had a long tail, on which Kennedy was sitting; and the hot weather would have caused the shirt to stick to the president's back. The hole in the shirt lined up almost exactly with the hole in the jacket.

The FBI calculated the angle from the easternmost sixth–floor window to Kennedy's upper back. After making allowances for the slight downward slope of the road, it was determined that any bullet fired between frame 210, the first instant at which a sixth–floor gunman could have seen Kennedy, and frame 225, when Kennedy can clearly be seen to be injured, would have travelled downward at an average angle of 17° 43′ 30″ to the horizontal.[20] With the shirt and jacket aligned normally, the holes are far too low for the hypothetical bullet to have come out of the throat at the required angle. The bullet holes would have had to be about four inches or ten centimetres higher, close to the level of the collars, as the Warren Commission discovered. The Commission was obliged to line up not only Kennedy's back and throat wounds, but also Connally's back wound. The Commission's own photographic reconstruction demonstrated that the only way this could be done was by placing Kennedy's back wound too high and his throat wound too low.[21] If one were able to look at the motorcade from directly above, it

19. For the timing of Willis's photograph, see Wrone, *op. cit.*, pp.119–120. For a clear reproduction of Willis's photograph, see Groden, *op. cit.*, p.24 and Josiah Thompson, *Six Seconds in Dallas: A Micro–Study of the Kennedy Assassination*, Bernard Geis Associates, 1967, p.223.
20. The distance and angle from the sixth–floor window to Kennedy: *WR*, p.106.
21. CE 903 (*WCHE*, vol.18, p.96).

is possible that a straight line could be drawn from the south-eastern corner of the TSBD, through Kennedy's non-fatal wounds and through Connally's. Looking at the motorcade from the side, however, it is clear that no such line can be drawn.

Because bullets can sometimes veer off in unexpected directions on striking an internal object after entering a body, it is conceivable, though unlikely, that a bullet from the sixth floor of the TSBD hit President Kennedy in the back, veered upward, and passed out of his throat. Unfortunately, a bullet following an upward trajectory could not have caused any of Governor Connally's injuries, as the single–bullet theory demanded. The unavoidable implication is that Kennedy's back and throat wounds were caused either by separate bullets or by one bullet fired from somewhere other than the sixth–floor window. It also follows that at least one further bullet is required in order to account for Connally's wounds.

Although some of the incontrovertible facts of the case appeared to implicate Oswald, other incontrovertible facts appeared to exculpate him: the time available for the shooting, the capabilities of the alleged weapon, and the nature of the injuries. These three factors came together to suggest strongly that the essential part of the Warren Commission's case, the single–bullet theory, was not only unsupported by the evidence but was actively contradicted by the evidence. The failure of the single–bullet theory proved that Oswald could not have committed the crime alone.

5 The Rifle, the Paraffin Tests, and the Magic Bullet

Not only was the Warren Commission unable to demonstrate that Oswald had committed the crime alone, but three important pieces of evidence showed that he had almost certainly not played any part in the shooting: the poor physical condition of the rifle; the absence of gunpowder residues on Oswald's right cheek; and the provenance of the bullet that was supposed to have passed through Kennedy and Connally.

The experts from the US Army and the FBI who had tested the rifle discovered that it was actually not usable in its original state. Ronald Simmons reported that the US Army marksmen under his command were obliged to apply shims to the telescopic sight before the rifle could be aimed: "They could not sight the weapon in using the telescope, and no attempt was made to sight it in using the iron sight. We did adjust the telescopic sight by the addition of two shims, one which tended to adjust the azimuth, and one which adjusted an elevation."[1] Even after the telescopic sight had been repaired, it proved unreliable and inaccurate. According to the FBI's firearms specialist, "Every time we changed the adjusting screws to move the crosshairs in the telescopic sight in one direction it also affected the movement of the impact or the point of impact in the other direction.... We fired several shots and found that the shots were not all landing in the same place, but were gradually moving away from the point of impact."[2] The condition

1. The need for shims: *WCHE*, vol.3, pp.443–444.
2. Problems with the telescopic sight: *WCHE*, vol.3, p.405.

of both the bolt and the trigger pull meant that the rifle could not be aimed accurately. Simmons reported that "There were several comments made — particularly with respect to the amount of effort required to open the bolt.... There was also comment made about the trigger pull ...in the first stage the trigger is relatively free, and it suddenly required a greater pull to actually fire the weapon.... The pressure to open the bolt was so great that that we tended to move the rifle off the target."[3] It is very unlikely that the rifle discovered on the sixth floor of the Texas School Book Depository could have caused any of the wounds to Kennedy, Connally or Tague, except by accident.

A few hours after the assassination, Oswald underwent a test that was routinely carried out on those suspected of having fired a gun. Liquid paraffin wax was spread on his hands and, because he was right–handed, his right cheek. When hardened, the paraffin wax would extract from deep in the pores of his skin any fine residues given off by the firing of a gun, even if he had washed his skin in the meantime.

Barium and antimony, which are found in gunpowder residues, are also found in several common substances such as printing ink, which Oswald certainly had handled on the morning of the assassination. The presence of these substances is not sufficient evidence of having fired a gun, but their absence is sufficient evidence of having not fired a gun. In other words, firing a gun would deposit barium and antimony on parts of the skin close to the gun. If barium and antimony were found on Oswald's skin, they may have been deposited by the firing of a gun. But they may instead have been deposited by other means; for example, they may have been deposited on his hands by the handling of books. If barium and antimony were not found on Oswald's cheek, he almost certainly did not fire a rifle.

Oswald's paraffin casts were subjected to two analyses. The standard chemical test, in which the casts are brought into contact with diphenylbenzidine, showed evidence of barium and antimony on Oswald's hands, but not on his cheek. According to an FBI memo, "The results show Punctate traces of nitrate found in the paraffin on the right and left hands consistent with that of a person

3. Problems with the bolt and the trigger mechanism: *WCHE*, vol.3, pp.449, 451.

who handled or fired a firearm. The paraffin of right check [*sic*] showed no traces of nitrate."[4]

The chemical test was used by many police departments, and was considered sufficiently reliable for criminal investigations, but in this case a more incisive test was also used. Neutron activation analysis, which is capable of identifying the presence of substances in quantities much too small to be captured by the diphenylbenzidine test, also showed no incriminating quantities of residues on Oswald's cheek. The result was reported in an internal Warren Commisssion memo: "At best, the analysis shows that Oswald may have fired a pistol, although this is by no means certain.... There is no basis for concluding that he also fired a rifle."[5] For the public record, the FBI's expert was led through a series of carefully rehearsed questions which allowed him to avoid specifying the quantities of barium and antimony discovered by neutron activation analysis, but which implied that the quantities on Oswald's cheek were so small as to be insignificant.[6] The presence of almost identical quantities of barium and antimony both on the inside of the cast, which had touched Oswald's cheek, and the outside, which had not, suggests that the cast had become contaminated. The results were complicated by the fact that the NAA tests were conducted later than the chemical test, which involved washing the casts. This has the effect of removing substantial amounts of barium and small amounts of antimony. The apparent contamination of the paraffin cast of Oswald's right cheek allowed the *Warren Report* unjustifiably to discard the evidence of the neutron activation analysis.[7]

In order to check the validity of the neutron activation analysis of Oswald's paraffin casts, a controlled test was made. Although the documents so far released to the public are incomplete, it appears that seven marksmen fired a rifle of the same type as that found on the sixth floor. The standard paraffin test was administered, and the paraffin casts were subjected to neutron activation analysis. All seven subjects showed substantial amounts of bar-

4. Result of chemical test: FBI HQ JFK Assassination File, 62–109060–8.
5. Memo from Redlich to Dulles, 2 July 1964, Investigation and Evidence File, RG 272, Series 12, box 4, folder 3, National Archives.
6. Questioning of John Gallagher: *WCHE*, vol.15, p.752.
7. *WR*, p.562, which incorrectly states that both of Oswald's hands tested negative.

ium and antimony on their hands and, more importantly, on their cheeks. Even after the control casts had undergone the same chemical treatment as Oswald's casts, they still displayed substantial amounts of both barium and antimony. The absence of significant quantities of residues on Oswald's cheek meant that he almost certainly had not fired a rifle that day.[8]

It was essential to the lone–gunman hypothesis that the single bullet which caused all the non–fatal wounds was the bullet known as Commission Exhibit 399. Robert Frazier, the FBI's firearms expert, claimed that the CE 399 bullet had been fired from the rifle found in the Texas School Book Depository.[9] If Frazier's identification of the CE 399 bullet with the rifle is correct, the bullet's association with the assassination cannot plausibly be accidental. There are three possibilities. The first is that the CE 399 bullet was fired from the sixth floor of the TSBD; it caused all the non–fatal injuries to President Kennedy and Governor Connally; and it was discovered on Connally's stretcher. In this case, the single–bullet theory is correct, and the lone–gunman hypothesis is plausible. Alternatively, the CE 399 bullet was fired from the sixth floor; it caused some, but not all, of the non–fatal injuries to President Kennedy and Governor Connally; and it was discovered on Connally's stretcher. In this case, the single–bullet theory is incorrect, and there was more than one gunman in Dealey Plaza. The other possibility is that the CE 399 bullet was not fired from the sixth floor during the assassination, and must have been inserted into evidence fraudulently, either before it was discovered on the stretcher or while it was in the possession of law enforcement officers.

Two aspects of the evidence suggest that at least some of the non–fatal wounds had not been caused by Commission Exhibit 399: the trajectory of the bullet, and the lack of damage to the bullet. Two other aspects suggest that the bullet was not authentic: the circumstances of the bullet's discovery, and its chain of possession.

8. See Harold Weisberg, *Post Mortem: JFK Assassination Cover–Up Smashed*, Weisberg, 1975, p.437. The results of the controlled test were made public two decades after the assassination as the result of a court case, and are available in the Harold Weisberg Archive, Hood College, Frederick, Maryland. The case was *Weisberg v. Energy Research and Development Administration and the Department of Justice*, Civil Action 75–226. See also Appendix B, Neutron Activation Analysis, p.117 below.
9. Robert Frazier: *WCHE*, vol.3, pp.421–428.

The known location of the bullet holes in President Kennedy's clothing show that the most likely location of the wound in Kennedy's back was lower than the wound in his throat. Photographs and home movies show that he was sitting almost upright during the latter stages of the motorcade. JFK's non–fatal injuries cannot all have been caused by one shot from the sixth floor of the TSBD, which was approximately 60 feet or 18 metres above the road. It is clear that the single–bullet theory cannot be correct and, consequently, that more than one gunman was involved in the shooting. If the CE 399 bullet is genuine, it must have been fired from the sixth floor, and must then have been discovered on Connally's stretcher. The bullet may have caused Connally's wounds, but cannot have done so after passing through Kennedy.

The CE 399 bullet had sustained only superficial damage. Its base was slightly flattened, and there were several fine scratches on the copper surface.[10] For the bullet to be considered genuine, its limited amount of damage must be consistent with the injuries the bullet is supposed to have caused. The Warren Commission, which was given the task of proving Lee Oswald's sole guilt, needed to demonstrate that CE 399 could have broken Governor Connally's rib and wrist bones while suffering no more than a slightly flattened base and a few scratches. Tests were carried out on behalf of the Warren Commission by the Department of Defense at Edgewood Arsenal in Maryland. Two experiments suggested strongly that the CE 399 bullet had not caused Connally's wounds. Bullets of the same type as CE 399 were fired into the wrist bones of ten human cadavers. All ten bullets were severely deformed, unlike CE 399. One bullet was fired into a goat's rib, and was flattened substantially more than CE 399. Another bullet was fired into a block of gelatin, and was only moderately flattened, like CE 399.[11] Dr Joseph Dolce, the US Army's most senior expert in wound ballistics, wrote to the House Select Committee on Assassinations that "one bullet striking the President's neck, the Governor's chest and

10. Photograph of CE 399: *WCHE*, vol.17, p.49.
11. Alfred G. Olivier and Arthur J. Dziemian, *Wound Ballistics of 6.5–mm Mannlicher–Carcano Ammunition*, Chemical Research and Development Laboratories Report 3264. The Edgewood Arsenal report was withheld from the public for ten years, and only made available as the result of a law suit under the Freedom of Information Act by the researcher Harold Weisberg.

wrist, should be badly deformed, as our experiments at the Edgewood Arsenal proved."[12]

According to the FBI's ballistics expert, Robert Frazier, the CE 399 bullet weighed 158.6 grains (10.277 grammes, or 0.363 ounces). He examined three unfired bullets of the same type as the CE 399 bullet, and found that they weighed 160.85, 161.5 and 161.1 grains. Frazier pointed out that CE 399's weight was within the normal range of intact bullets, and that "there did not necessarily have to be any weight loss to the bullet."[13]

Some metal was missing from the CE 399 bullet for reasons other than the bullet striking Kennedy and Connally. The bullet had been fired from a rifle, which would have removed approximately half a grain from the copper coating. The FBI had taken two small samples from the bullet: one from the copper at its nose, and one from the lead at its base.

If CE 399 were the only bullet to have struck Governor Connally, it must have been the source of all the metal fragments that were deposited in his chest, thigh and wrist wounds. Two small fragments were removed from his wrist.[14] The larger of the two fragments weighed 0.5 grain.[15] Dr Charles Gregory, who operated on Connally's wrist, pointed out that other fragments were removed from the wrist and then mislaid: "there were two fragments of metal retrieved . . . the major one or ones now being missing."[16] A nurse, Audrey Bell, also recalled several missing fragments.[17] A fragment measuring approximately 2 mm by 0.5 mm was removed from just below the skin on the thigh.[18] Other fragments were left in place. According to Dr Robert Shaw, who had operated on Connally, "more than three grains of metal [remained] in the wrist."[19] A small fragment remained in the chest.[20] A flake of metal measuring approximately 2 mm by 0.2 mm remained embedded in

12. Dr Dolce's letter is available at the National Archives: NARA RIF no. 180–10084–10430. Dr Dolce was not called to testify before the Warren Commission.
13. Robert Frazier: *WCHE*, vol.3, p.430.
14. Fragments from wrist: CE 842 (*WCHE*, vol.17, p.841).
15. Weight of fragment: *WCHE*, vol.5, p.72.
16. Dr Charles Gregory: *WCHE*, vol.4, p.123.
17. Audrey Bell: ARRB Medical Document 184, pp.2–3.
18. Fragment from thigh: *WCHE*, vol.4, p.125.
19. Dr Robert Shaw: *WCHE*, vol.4, p.113.
20. Fragment in chest: *WCHE*, vol.6, p.111.

Connally's femur.[21]

The pathologists who conducted President Kennedy's autopsy were presented with the CE 399 bullet by representatives of the Warren Commission and were asked whether they thought it could have caused Connally's injuries. Dr James Humes, the chief pathologist, replied:

> I think that is most unlikely.... This missile is basically intact; its jacket appears to me to be intact, and I do not understand how it could possibly have left fragments in either of those locations.... I doubt if this missile would have left behind it any metallic fragments from its physical appearance at this time.... Metallic fragments were not removed and are still present in Governor Connally's thigh. I can't conceive of where they came from this missile.[22]

The other two pathologists, Dr J. Thornton Boswell and Dr Pierre Finck, who stated that "there are too many fragments," agreed with Dr Humes.[23]

IF CE 399 was the bullet which had passed through Kennedy and Connally, it must have been discovered either on Connally's person or on his stretcher. A bullet was in fact discovered on a stretcher. Darrell Tomlinson, an engineer at Parkland Hospital in Dallas, was working on an elevator close to the operating theatre in which Governor Connally was undergoing emergency surgery. He moved one of two nearby unoccupied stretchers, and noticed a bullet roll off the stretcher and onto the floor. He alerted the hospital's chief of personnel, a retired police officer named O.P. Wright, who picked up the bullet and handed it to a representative of the Secret Service.

One of the two stretchers outside the elevator may have been Connally's. Arlen Specter, counsel for the Warren Commission, pressed Darrell Tomlinson to specify that the stretcher that may

21. Metal in femur: *WCHE*, vol.4, p.125.
22. Dr James Humes: *WCHE*, vol.2, pp.374–376.
23. Dr J. Thornton Boswell: *WCHE*, vol.2, p.377. Dr Pierre Finck: *WCHE*, vol.2, pp.381–382.

have contained Connally was the one that had contained the bullet. Tomlinson refused to do so.[24]

The only evidence about the location of the bullet was the testimony of Darrell Tomlinson. O.P. Wright was not called to testify before the Warren Commission. Nevertheless, the *Warren Report* stated categorically that:

> A nearly whole bullet was found on Governor Connally's stretcher at Parkland Hospital after the assassination.... The Commission has concluded that the bullet came from the Governor's stretcher. That conclusion is buttressed by evidence which eliminated President Kennedy's stretcher as a source of the bullet. President Kennedy remained on the stretcher on which he was carried into the hospital.... He was never removed from the stretcher.[25]

It is certainly true that the bullet could not have come from Kennedy's stretcher, which remained in a different part of the hospital until after the bullet was discovered, but it is far from certain that the bullet came from Connally's stretcher.

According to an FBI memo of 7 July 1964, both Tomlinson and Wright had been shown Commission Exhibit 399, and both men had tentatively identified it as the bullet they had seen in Parkland Hospital. The CE 399 bullet was referred to by the FBI's original identification number, Exhibit C1:

> On June 12, 1964, Darrell C. Tomlinson, Maintenance Employee, Parkland Hospital, Dallas, Texas, was shown Exhibit C1, a rifle slug, by Special Agent Bardwell D. Odum, Federal Bureau of Investigation. Tomlinson stated it appears to be the same one he found on a hospital carriage at Parkland Hospital on November 22, 1963, but he cannot positively identify the bullet as the one he found and showed to Mr O.P. Wright.... On June 12, 1964, O.P. Wright, Personnel Officer, Parkland Hospital, Dallas, Texas, advised Special Agent Bardwell D.

24. Darrell Tomlinson: *WCHE*, vol.6, pp.130–134.
25. *WR*, pp.79–81.

> Odum that Exhibit C1, a rifle slug, shown to him at the time of the interview, looks like the slug found at Parkland Hospital on November 22, 1963.... He advised he could not positively identify C1 as being the same bullet which was found on November 22, 1963.[26]

There are, however, reasons to disbelieve the 7 July memo. In his appearance before the Warren Commission, Tomlinson was not shown the CE 399 bullet, and was not asked to identify it as the bullet he had discovered. Wright had not given evidence. A private researcher, Josiah Thompson, tracked down Wright in November 1966 and asked him about the bullet. In the presence of two witnesses, Wright replied that the bullet he had seen possessed a pointed tip rather than the rounded tip of the CE 399 bullet.[27] Wright's assertion that CE 399 was not the bullet he had seen was supported by another FBI memo, dated 20 June 1964 and declassified several decades after the assassination: "neither DARRELL C. TOMLINSON ... nor O.P. WRIGHT ... can identify bullet."[28] The 7 July memo was contradicted also by Bardwell D. Odum, the FBI agent who, according to the memo, showed CE 399 to Tomlinson and Wright. Odum was interviewed by Josiah Thompson and another researcher, and denied that he had handled the CE 399 bullet: "I didn't show it to anybody at Parkland. I didn't have any bullet ... I don't think I ever saw it even."[29]

The bullet passed through several hands *en route* to the FBI laboratory: Darrell Tomlinson spotted a bullet, and alerted O.P. Wright; O.P Wright picked up the bullet and gave it to Richard Johnsen, one of the Secret Service agents stationed in Parkland Hospital immediately after the assassination; Johnsen showed the bullet to Gerald Behn, the head of the Secret Service's White House detail, probably on the evening of 22 November; Johnsen or Behn appears to have handed the bullet to James Rowley, the chief of the Secret Service; Rowley gave the bullet to Elmer Todd of the FBI's Washington of-

26. Identification of CE 399: CE 2011, p.2 (*WCHE*, vol.24, p.412).
27. Josiah Thompson, *Six Seconds in Dallas: a Micro–Study of the Kennedy Assassination*, New York: Bernard Geis Associates, 1967, p.175.
28. Shanklin to Hoover, 20 June 1964, FBI Dallas File 100–10461.
29. Gary Aguilar and Josiah Thompson, 'The Magic Bullet: Even More Magical Than We Knew,' at http://history-matters.com/essays/frameup/EvenMoreMagical/EvenMoreMagical.htm.

fice; Todd inscribed his initials on the bullet and gave it to Robert Frazier of the FBI laboratory, who also initialled the bullet.[30]

The Warren Commission asked the FBI in May 1964 to attempt to authenticate the chain of possession of several items of evidence, including Commission Exhibit 399. The FBI was unable to account for the early stages of the bullet's journey. Tomlinson "cannot positively identify the bullet." Wright "could not positively identify C1 as being the same bullet." Johnsen "could not identify this bullet." Behn does not appear to have been asked to identify the bullet. Rowley "could not identify this bullet." Only Todd and Frazier, who had initialled the bullet, were able to identify CE 399 as the bullet they had handled on the evening of the assassination.[31]

Commission Exhibit 399 is an essential component of the case against Lee Harvey Oswald as the lone assassin of President Kennedy. Because the bullet had been fired from the rifle apparently owned by Oswald, the bullet's connection to the JFK assassination cannot be accidental: either it was genuine, and had been fired during the assassination, or it had not been fired during the assassination, and was planted. The almost impossible trajectory required by the single bullet theory shows that CE 399 is extremely unlikely to have passed through both President Kennedy and Governor Connally. The lack of damage to CE 399 implies that it did not cause all of Connally's injuries. These factors, as well as the bullet's patchy chain of possession and the strong likelihood that it is not the bullet that had been discovered in Parkland Hospital, makes it difficult to avoid the conclusion that Commission Exhibit 399 was entered into evidence fraudulently after the assassination, while it was in the possession of law enforcement officers.

30. Wright to Johnsen: CE 1024 (*WCHE*, vol.18, pp.799–800). Rowley to Todd: CE 2011, p.2 (*WCHE*, vol.24, p.412). Todd to Frazier: *WCHE*, vol.3, p.428.
31. Identification of CE 399: CE 2011, p.2 (*WCHE*, vol.24, p.412).

6 Lee Harvey Oswald's Motive

Only a small part of the *Warren Report* dealt with the facts of the JFK assassination. The majority of the 900–page *Report* was devoted to a biography of Oswald, in an effort to show that he was capable of doing what he was supposed to have done. Despite this effort, the Commission was unable to find any evidence of a political or ideological motive.

All the evidence in fact pointed the other way. Oswald had repeatedly expressed his admiration for President Kennedy both as an individual and as a politician. Michael Paine, who took Oswald to a meeting of the American Civil Liberties Union, claimed that Oswald "thought President Kennedy was doing quite a good job in civil rights, which was high praise coming from Lee."[1] Lillian Murret, Oswald's aunt, reported Oswald's opinion of Kennedy: "he said he liked him."[2] Samuel Ballen, who interviewed Oswald for a job, stated that "I just can't see his having any venom towards President Kennedy . . . this is an individual who felt warmly towards President Kennedy."[3] Paul Gregory, a speaker of Russian who knew the Oswald family in Dallas, said that Oswald "expressed admiration of Kennedy. . . . I never heard him say anything derogatory about Kennedy. He seemed to admire the man . . . he always expressed what I would interpret as admiration for Kennedy . . . I remember in their apartment that we did look at this picture of Kennedy, and Marina said, 'He looks like a nice young man,' and

1. Michael Paine: *WCHE*, vol.2, p.399.
2. Lillian Murret: *WCHE*, vol.8, p.153; Marilyn Murret, Lillian's daughter and Oswald's cousin, did not think that Oswald had the capability or motivation to kill Kennedy: *WCHE*, vol.8, pp.176–177.
3. Samuel Ballen: *WCHE*, vol.9, p.48.

Lee said something, yes, he is a good leader, or something, as I remember, [it] was a positive remark about Kennedy."[4] George de Mohrenschildt, who befriended the Oswalds, claimed that Oswald "was an admirer of President Kennedy.... I mentioned to him that ... I thought that Kennedy was doing a very good job.... And he also agreed with me: 'Yes, yes, yes; I think [he] is an excellent President, young, full of energy, full of good ideas."[5]

The *Warren Report* offered a vague psychological explanation:

> Clues to Oswald's motives can be found in his family history, his education or lack of it, his acts, his writings, and the recollections of those who had close contacts with him throughout his life....
>
> The Commission could not make any definitive determination of Oswald's motives. It has endeavored to isolate factors which contributed to his character and which might have influenced his decision to assassinate President Kennedy. These factors were:
>
> 1. His deep–rooted resentment of all authority which was expressed in a hostility toward every society in which he lived;
> 2. His inability to enter into meaningful relationships with people, and a continuous pattern of rejecting his environment in favor of new surroundings;
> 3. His urge to try to find a place in history and despair at times over failures in his various undertakings;
> 4. His capacity for violence as evidenced by his attempt to kill General Walker;
> 5. His avowed commitment to Marxism and communism, as he understood the terms and developed his own interpretation of them; this was expressed by his antagonism toward the United States, by his

4. Paul Gregory: *WCHE*, vol.9, p.148.

5. George de Mohrenschildt: *WCHE*, vol.9, p.255. For more about de Mohrenschildt and the Oswalds, see George de Mohrenschildt, ed. Michael Rinella, *Lee Harvey Oswald As I Knew Him*, University Press of Kansas, 2014.

> defection to the Soviet Union, by his failure to be reconciled with life in the United States even after his disenchantment with the Soviet Union, and by his efforts, though frustrated, to go to Cuba.
>
> Each of these contributed to his capacity to risk all in cruel and irresponsible actions.[6]

A closer look at the *Warren Report*'s five factors which "might have influenced his decision" to kill Kennedy shows that most of them are contradicted by the evidence.

The first claim is that Oswald had a "deep–rooted resentment of all authority which was expressed in a hostility toward every society in which he lived." Oswald seems to have had no more than an occasional vague distrust of authority. He had been a relatively obedient member of the Marines for several years. His well–documented behaviour in New Orleans in the summer of 1963, together with other aspects of his interesting career, shows little evidence of anti–authoritarian impulses.[7]

The second claim, that Oswald had an "inability to enter into meaningful relationships with people," was based partly on Oswald's lack of effort to get to know his fellow employees during the five weeks he spent at the Texas School Book Depository. The fact that Oswald was married with two young children shows clearly that he did not have an "inability to enter into meaningful relationships with people."

The third claim involved Oswald's "urge to try to find a place in history and despair at times over failures in his various undertakings." This seems to be the motive that the Warren Commissioners themselves found the most persuasive. After the final meeting of the Commission, one of its members, Senator Richard Russell, was asked by President Johnson about Oswald's motive. Russell replied that "he was a general misanthropic fellow . . . he had a desire to get his name in history and all."[8] Newspaper and television commentators in the decades since the assassination have consistently favoured this interpretation. There is, however, no evidence

6. *WR*, pp.22–23.
7. See Chapter 9, The Career of Lee Harvey Oswald, p.71 below.
8. Lyndon Johnson to Richard Russell, White House Telephone Transcripts, 18 September 1964, LBJ Library, Austin, Texas.

to support it. Oswald himself never expressed a "desire to get his name in history and all." Nor did he ever boast of killing President Kennedy or Officer Tippit. On the contrary, throughout the two days he spent in police custody Oswald consistently denied any involvement in the murders, famously claiming that "I'm just a patsy."[9] Even in his last conscious moments, he refused to take credit for the assassination. A policeman, B.H. Combest, attempted to obtain a confession after Oswald had been shot by Jack Ruby:

> I laid him down on the floor and removed the handcuffs that he had on him.... I told him was there anything that he wanted me to tell anybody or was there anything he wanted to say right now before it was too late ... trying to let him know if he was ever going to say anything he was going to have to say it then.... [Oswald] just shook his head and I said, "Do you have anything you want to tell us now," and he shook his head.... I kept talking to him as long as I thought he would try to answer me, hoping that he would give a dying declaration on the shooting.[10]

The fourth claim noted Oswald's "capacity for violence as evidenced by his attempt to kill General Walker." Oswald was almost certainly not one of the two men who attempted to shoot General Edwin Walker in April 1963. The only witness claimed that neither of the two men resembled Oswald, and that the men drove away in separate cars. Oswald could not drive.[11] The strongest evidence against Oswald was provided by his widow, Marina, who claimed that he had admitted to her that he had shot at Walker and that on the evening of the shooting he had left a handwritten note explaining what she should do if he were arrested.[12] Lee Oswald's note does not in fact link him to the Walker shooting: it is not dated, not signed, and does not mention Walker.[13] Marina Oswald's statement was obtained under duress, while she was being interrogated

9. The notebook of a reporter, Seth Kantor: *WCHE*, vol.20, p.366.
10. B.H. Combest: *WCHE*, vol.12, p.185.
11. For the Warren Commission's case that Oswald shot at Walker, see *WR*, pp.183–187. Walter Kirk Coleman: CE 2001 (*WCHE*, vol.24, pp.40–41) and CE 2958 (*WCHE*, vol.26, pp.437–441). For Oswald's driving, see p.69 below.
12. Marina Oswald's account: *WR*, pp.405–406.
13. Oswald's note: CE 1 (*WCHE*, vol.16, pp.1–2).

by the Secret Service and the FBI and threatened with deportation back to the Soviet Union.[14] She also felt obliged to incriminate her late husband in other areas. In her earliest statements to the FBI and the Secret Service, she claimed that Oswald had not practised firing a rifle, but she later changed her mind and told her interrogators what they wanted to hear: "I said before I had never seen it before. But I think you understand. I want to help you, and that is why there is no reason for concealing anything. I will not be charged with anything."[15] She then told the FBI that Oswald had practised with his rifle in January 1963. On learning that Oswald had not in fact bought the rifle until two months later, she admitted that "she had been mistaken" and that she only "deduced that he might have been practicing with the rifle."[16]

The Warren Commission relied on Marina Oswald's statements despite being aware that they were contradictory and unreliable. One of the Commission's attorneys, Norman Redlich, wrote in a memo to J. Lee Rankin that "neither you nor I have any desire to smear the reputation of any individual. We cannot ignore, however, that Marina Oswald has repeatedly lied to the [Secret] Service, the FBI, and this Commission on matters which are of vital concern to the people of this country and the world."[17] Redlich expanded on this when testifying before the HSCA: "She may not have told the truth in connection with the attempted killing of General Walker.... I gave to Mr Rankin a lengthy document.... I indicated the testimony that she had given, the instances where it was in conflict."[18]

General Walker himself pointed out that the bullet which had almost killed him was not the same type as the bullets fired in the JFK assassination, and thus cannot have been fired from the only rifle which could be attributed to Oswald. Walker also claimed that the bullet which the Warren Commission entered into evidence was not the bullet he had handled at the time of the shoot-

14. Marina Oswald's treatment: *WCHE*, vol.1, p.410.

15. Oswald had not practised firing a rifle: CE 1401 (*WCHE*, vol.22, p.763) and CE 1403 (*WCHE*, vol.22, p.778). "I want to help you": *WCHE*, vol.1, pp.14–15.

16. Practising in January 1963: CE 1156 (*WCHE*, vol.22, p.197). "She had been mistaken": CE 1404 (*WCHE*, p.785). The rifle had been purchased by 'A. Hidell' in March 1963: *WR*, p.119.

17. Redlich's memo: *HSCA Appendix*, vol.11, p.126.

18. Redlich's testimony: *ibid.*, p.127.

ing.[19] The Dallas police had claimed in April 1963 that the attempt on Walker involved one steel–jacketed 30.06–calibre bullet, fired from a high–powered rifle. General Walker, who had examined the surviving bullet fragment, agreed. The only rifle and bullets associated with Oswald were of a different type and size. Tests showed that the fragment was made of a lead alloy different from that in the bullet fragments found in President Kennedy's car.[20] These tests were later contradicted by neutron activation analysis done for the House Select Committee on Assassinations, but that evidence in turn has been contradicted by later research, which demonstrates that neutron activation analysis is incapable of determining the origin of bullet fragments.[21]

The fifth claim involved Oswald's "avowed commitment to Marxism and communism," a commitment difficult to reconcile with his surviving notes for a speech that he gave to a college in Alabama in the summer of 1963.[22] In the notes, Oswald has little good to say about communism or communists, whom he describes as "a pitiful bunch." He criticises both the Soviet system and western capitalism, but those criticisms are not much different from the opinions of most reasonable people, and do not illustrate any "deep–rooted resentment."

The Warren Commission went out of its way to conclude that Oswald's motives were purely psychological, and that even though he possessed an "avowed commitment to Marxism and communism," the alleged assassin was not part of a communist conspiracy. Indeed, the Commission was set up precisely to defuse rumours of a communist conspiracy, rumours which were based in part on a visit which Lee Harvey Oswald appears to have made to Mexico City a few weeks before the assassination.

19. Photograph of the bullet: CE 573 (*WCHE*, vol.7, p.390). See Justice Department Criminal Division File 62–117290–1473 for Walker's correspondence with the Justice Department on this matter.
20. Bullet tests: FBI HQ Oswald File, 62–109060–22.
21. *HSCA Appendix*, vol.1, p.502. See Appendix B, Neutron Activation Analysis, p.117 below.
22. Notes for a speech: CE 102 (*WCHE*, vol.16, pp.441–442). A summary of Oswald's speech, as it was recalled by Robert Fitzpatrick and other members of the audience: CE 2649, pp.10–17 (*WCHE*, vol.25, pp.924–928).

7 "A Little Incident in Mexico City"

Lee Harvey Oswald was arrested less than an hour and a half after the assassination of President Kennedy. Very soon after his arrest, several pieces of background information reached government circles in Washington. Oswald, a self–declared Marxist and former Marine, had defected to the Soviet Union in 1959. He had threatened to renounce his US citizenship and to pass on secrets he had obtained while working as a radar operator for the U2 spy plane operation. He had returned to the US in 1962.[1] Between 27 September and 3 October 1963, Oswald had been in Mexico City, where he had contacted the Soviet Embassy and the Cuban Consulate several times by telephone and at least five times in person.[2]

The Soviet and Cuban diplomatic compounds in Mexico City were being thoroughly monitored by the CIA, which possessed tape recordings and transcripts of Oswald's telephone calls, as well as photographs of Oswald as he went in and out. According to Winston Scott, the head of the CIA station in Mexico City, "persons watching these embassies photographed OSWALD as he entered and left each one; and clocked the time he spent on each visit."[3] Contrary to certain official sources, the CIA's Mexico City station

1. *WR*, p.655.

2. *WR*, p.658. For a detailed account of Oswald's visit to Mexico City, see John Newman, *Oswald and the CIA*, Carroll and Graf, 1995, pp.352–391; and Bill Simpich, *State Secret: Wiretapping in Mexico City, Double Agents, and the Framing of Lee Oswald*, at http://www.maryferrell.org/wiki/index.php/State_Secret_Preface, especially chapters 4 and 5.

3. Russ Holmes Work File, 104–10419–10314, p.11, NARA. For the extent of the CIA's surveillance, see *Lopez Report*, p.27.

knew about Oswald's visits to the Cuban Consulate before the assassination, and passed this information to headquarters. Scott stated that

> every piece of information concerning Lee Harvey Oswald was reported immediately after it was received to: US Ambassador Thomas C. Mann, by memorandum; the FBI Chief in Mexico, by memorandum; and to my headquarters by cable; and included in each and every one of these reports was the conversation Oswald had, so far as it was known. These reports were made on all his contacts with both the Cuban Consulate and with the Soviets.[4]

Oswald had applied for a visa to allow him to visit Cuba, and had enquired about obtaining a visa to visit the Soviet Union. More ominously, he had met and spoken by telephone to Valeriy Kostikov, a Soviet diplomat who was suspected by the CIA of being an agent attached to the KGB's Department 13, which was in charge of assassinations and sabotage.[5] The obvious implication was that the man accused of assassinating President Kennedy was in some way associated with the Soviet or Cuban regimes. This implication was strengthened when the FBI discovered shortly after the assassination that, two weeks earlier, it had intercepted a letter apparently sent by Oswald to the Soviet Embassy in Washington, in which he claimed that he had met Kostikov in Mexico City.[6]

The FBI learned on the afternoon of the assassination that it had not been kept fully informed by the CIA of Oswald's activities in Mexico City. To remedy this, two sets of evidence were sent by the CIA station in Mexico City to the FBI in Dallas, arriving early on the morning of 23 November: at least one tape recording of a phone call by a man claiming to be Oswald, and several photographs of the only non–Hispanic man to enter the Soviet compound on

4. Winston Scott, *Foul Foe*, pp.268–269, quoted in Newman, *op. cit.*, p.416.
5. For Oswald's dealings with Kostikov, see Newman, *op. cit.*, pp.356–362. CIA memo linking Kostikov with the KGB's sabotage and assassinations department: NARA RIF no. 104–10436–10025.
6. Although the letter (CE 15 [*WCHE*, vol.16, p.33]) refers to "Kostin", it is widely assumed that "Kostin" was in fact Kostikov; see *WR*, p.309.

the date of Oswald's meeting there with Kostikov.[7] FBI agents in Dallas made an unexpected and ominous discovery: neither the voice on the recording nor the man in the photographs matched the man who was in custody. Someone had impersonated Oswald in Mexico City. J. Edgar Hoover gave the news to President Johnson early on the morning after the assassination:

> We have up here the tape and the photograph of the man who was at the Soviet Embassy, using Oswald's name. That picture and the tape do not correspond to this man's voice, nor to his appearance. In other words, it appears that there is a second person who was at the Soviet Embassy down there.[8]

As a result of a conversation later that day between Gordon Shanklin, the agent in charge of the FBI's office in Dallas, and Alan Belmont, Assistant Director of the FBI, Hoover reported the evidence of an impostor to the head of the Secret Service:

> The Central Intelligence Agency advised that on October 1, 1963, an extremely sensitive source had reported that an individual identified himself as Lee Oswald, who contacted the Soviet Embassy in Mexico City inquiring as to any messages. Special Agents of this Bureau, who have conversed with Oswald in Dallas, Tex., have observed photographs of the individual referred to above and have listened to a recording of his voice. These Special Agents are of the opinion that the above–referred–to individual was not Lee Harvey Oswald.[9]

7. One photograph was published by the Warren Commission: *WCHE*, vol.20, p.691. Several others have since been widely published; see e.g. Robert Groden, *The Search for Lee Harvey Oswald*, Viking Penguin, 1995, pp.245–249.

8. Johnson to Hoover, White House Telephone Transcripts, 23 November 1963, 10:01am, LBJ Library, Austin, Texas. The recording of this call was erased, and a transcript survived only by luck; see Rex Bradford, 'The Fourteen Minute Gap,' at http://www.history-matters.com/essays/frameup/FourteenMinuteGap/FourteenMinuteGap.htm.

9. *HSCA Report*, pp.249–250. The phrase, "extremely sensitive source," presumably refers to the wiretaps and photographic surveillance. For Shanklin and Belmont, see *Lopez Report*, Addendum to Footnote 614, pp.11–12.

There is good evidence that Oswald had in fact made at least one visit to the Cuban Consulate and one to the Soviet Embassy. Oswald's Cuban visa application form, dated 27 September 1963, contains his signature and photograph, and must have been obtained from the Cuban Consulate. Valeriy Kostikov believed that he met the real Oswald at the Soviet Embassy on 27 September, according to the memoirs of his vice–consul.[10] Against this, HSCA investigators were told by CIA assets who had worked inside the Cuban Consulate that the majority of the employees within the consulate doubted that Oswald had visited the building.[11]

Whether or not the real Oswald had actually been present in Mexico City, several other encounters provided strong evidence that he had been impersonated. In two telephone calls to the Soviet Embassy, a man claiming to be Lee Harvey Oswald spoke "terrible, hardly recognizable Russian," according to the CIA's translator. Oswald himself spoke Russian very well.[12] The man who made the incriminating phone call to Kostikov had also phoned from the Cuban Consulate three days earlier, on Saturday 28 September. In this instance, not only was Oswald impersonated but the phone call or the transcript appear to have been fabricated. The Cuban Consulate and the switchboard at the Soviet Embassy were closed on Saturdays. Silvia Tirado de Durán, an employee at the Cuban Consulate who was mentioned by name in the transcript, denied that she had taken part in the call on the 28th.[13]

It is unclear whether the man in the photographs was the man who was claiming to be Oswald. At least one of the photographs was taken after the impersonation was over and Oswald was known to be in the US. Silvia Durán and Eusebio Azcue López, the Cuban

10. Oswald's Cuban visa application form: CE 2564 (*WCHE*, vol.25, pp.814). For Kostikov, see Newman, *op. cit.*, p.355.
11. Gaeton Fonzi, *The Last Investigation*, Thunder's Mouth Press, 1993, p.294.
12. "Terrible, hardly recognizable Russian": NARA RIF no. 104–10052–10084. For Oswald's language skills, see p.73 below. Three other phone calls, made on 27 September, in which a fluent Spanish speaker enquired about obtaining a visa to visit the Soviet Union, were originally thought to have been the work of an impostor. Because Oswald knew very little Spanish, and the speaker does not mention Oswald by name, these calls are now generally considered not to have any relevance to the Oswald case. For a list of all the phone calls, see *Lopez Report*, p.117.
13. For a transcript and discussion of the 28 September phone call, see Newman, *op. cit.*, pp.364–368, and Simpich, *op. cit.*, chapter 5, available at http://www.maryferrell.org/wiki/index.php/Featured_State_Secret_Chapter5.

Consul General, who between them had had at least three encounters with a man who claimed to be Oswald, each recalled that the man they had met looked nothing like either the real Oswald or the man in the photographs.[14]

Oswald's apparent contacts with the Soviet and Cuban representatives in Mexico City were reported by the news media, and gave rise to two competing conspiracy theories: either the assassination was the result of a communist conspiracy, or it was a conspiracy by elements sympathetic to the US state to blame the Soviet or Cuban regimes. The details of Oswald's impersonation, on the other hand, were kept secret from the general public. The impersonation was first documented in the House Select Committee on Assassinations' *Lopez Report* in 1978. The *Lopez Report* was only made available to the public in 1993, and even then several passages were withheld. The censored material included "another section of this final report dealing with whether or not Lee Oswald was an agent or asset of the Central Intelligence Agency."[15]

The transcripts and recordings of the telephone calls were tightly controlled by the CIA station in Mexico City, and most of the recordings appear to have been erased within a short time of the assassination. The telephone calls now survive only as transcripts. One call, in which an English–speaking man identifies himself as Lee Oswald, no longer exists even as a transcript.[16] The Mexico City station implied on 24 November that all the recordings, both originals and duplicates, had been destroyed before the assassination: "Regret complete recheck shows tapes for this period already erased."[17] Documents released three decades later show that this was not the case. An internal FBI cable, dated 25 November 1963, acknowledged the existence of the recordings: "If tapes covering any contacts subject [Oswald] with Soviet or Cuban embassies available forward to Bureau for laboratory examination and analysis together with transcript. Include tapes previously reviewed Dallas if they were returned to you."[18] At least one recording ex-

14. For Durán and Eusebio Azcue López see Fonzi, *op. cit.*, pp.289–290, and *HSCA Appendix*, vol.3, p.136.

15. *Lopez Report*, p.142. The *Warren Report*'s necessarily incomplete account of Oswald in Mexico City can be found on pp.658–659 and pp.730–736.

16. Newman, *op. cit.*, pp.369–375.

17. Claims that tapes had been erased: *Lopez Report*, p.164.

18. NARA RIF no. 124–10230–10434.

isted as late as April 1964, when it was listened to by a representative of the Warren Commission.[19] It is conceivable that transcripts rather than tapes were sent to Dallas, as was claimed by the FBI's legal attaché on 25 November, and that the FBI agents in Dallas actually listened to a recording over the phone, but it is certain that not all the tapes had been erased before the assassination.[20] The HSCA interviewed four of the seven FBI agents who had spoken to Oswald, but did not resolve the question of whether or not tapes had been sent to Dallas. Its *Report* merely stated the uncontroversial fact that these agents "had never listened to a recording of Oswald's voice."[21]

J. Edgar Hoover, Lyndon Johnson, and other Washington insiders were aware of the impersonation, and of its implications, early on the day after the assassination. It was clear that there was no innocent explanation: either Oswald had had at least one accomplice in Mexico City, or he had been impersonated without his knowledge. Either he was working for the Soviet or Cuban regimes, or he had been manipulated in order to implicate those regimes in Kennedy's assassination.

The existence of an impostor in Mexico City both undermined the idea that Oswald alone had killed President Kennedy, and turned the idea into a solid political necessity. The conspiracy in Mexico City involved Oswald, either as a member or as a victim. The apparent association between Oswald and Kostikov implied that the conspiracy was connected to the assassination of President Kennedy. The notion that Oswald, despite being centrally involved in this conspiracy, had actually planned and carried out the assassination all by himself, was surely recognised in Washington to require far too much of a coincidence to be credible.

It was clear to knowledgeable insiders that each of the competing conspiracy theories created a severe threat to public trust in established political institutions: either the US security system had failed to prevent a communist conspiracy, or some elements of the

19. For the existence of the tapes after the assassination, see *Lopez Report*, pp.168–169; Fonzi, *op. cit.*, pp.286–287; G.J. Rowell, 'Belin's Blooper,' *The Third Decade*, vol.4 no.2 (January 1988), pp.7–11; and ARRB, CIA Testimony, p.147. For the system of making duplicates and transcripts, see *ibid.*, p.144.
20. Transcripts, not tapes: *Lopez Report*, Addendum to Footnote 614, p.12.
21. *HSCA Report*, p.250.

US security system were complicit in the assassination.

Although, as Hoover put it, the evidence against Oswald was "not very, very strong ... the case as it stands now isn't strong enough to be able to get a conviction,"[22] the lone–nut explanation became the only expedient solution to a serious political problem. Once Oswald himself was murdered, and the burden of proof dramatically reduced, it became practicable to avoid an honest investigation into the assassination. A report was commissioned from the FBI, but the news media felt that it would be unable to convince the public of Oswald's guilt without having a more objective source on which to rely. The Warren Commission was set up, and was given the task of endorsing the idea that Oswald, acting for inscrutable personal motives, had been the lone assassin. The Commission proceeded to assemble a case for the prosecution. The print and broadcast media gave the *Warren Report* a huge amount of almost entirely uncritical coverage, and the political institutions survived.[23]

The apparent collusion between Oswald and the Soviet and Cuban regimes, if established, would have led to pressure for military retaliation. The need to defuse the danger of a nuclear war provided President Johnson with a bargaining tool. When pressing the reluctant Senator Richard Russell to serve on the Warren Commission, Johnson mentioned how he had managed to persuade the equally reluctant Earl Warren to play his part in promoting the lone–nut solution:

> Warren told me he wouldn't do it under any circumstances ... wouldn't have anything to do with it ... and I said let me read you one report ... and I said OK ... there's a million Americans involved here ... I just pulled out what Hoover told me about a little incident in Mexico City.... And he started crying and said, well I won't turn you down ... I'll just do whatever you say.[24]

22. Johnson to Hoover, White House Telephone Transcripts, 23 November 1963, 10:01am, LBJ Library, Austin, Texas.
23. The FBI report (CD 1) turned out to be extremely superficial; it spent only 200 words on the details of the assassination, and failed to mention all of the wounds. For the Warren Commission as a political tool and a public relations exercise, see p.6 above.
24. Johnson to Russell, White House Telephone Transcripts, 29 November 1963,

Many years later, it became clear that deliberate deception had taken place. When the CIA station in Mexico City sent the photographs to the FBI in Dallas, individuals within the station had known for several weeks that the man depicted was not Oswald. The station was able to compare photographs of the real Oswald with those of the impostor. Photographs were taken of every foreign visitor entering and leaving the diplomatic compounds.[25] The real Oswald seems to have made at least one visit to each compound, and so must have been photographed at least four times. The *Lopez Report* concluded that, contrary to early official claims, there was almost no chance that Oswald's visits would have been missed by the cameras.[26] On 26 September, the day before Oswald arrived in Mexico City, the cameras were tested and were working correctly.[27] Several CIA employees believed that photographs of Oswald existed. The chairman of the HSCA, Louis Stokes, alleged in 1978 that the CIA was withholding photographs of Oswald.[28] Along with the recordings of the phone calls, the photographs of Oswald at the compounds appear no longer to exist.

As well as possessing photographs of the real Oswald, the CIA's Mexico City station had been told by headquarters that the man in the photographs sent by Mexico City to headquarters was not Oswald. On 9 October, a few days after the photographs were taken, the station alerted CIA headquarters to the visit of the man claiming to be Oswald: "Have photos male appears be American entering Sovemb 1216 hours, leaving 1222 on 1 Oct. apparent age 35, athletic build, circa 6 feet, receding hairline." Headquarters consulted the genuine photographs and personal information in its file on the defector. It replied by cable the next day, stating that, on the contrary, the 23–year–old "Oswald is five feet ten inches, one hundred sixty–five pounds, light brown wavy hair, blue eyes." Despite sending this relatively accurate description to Mexico City, CIA headquarters passed on the incorrect description to the FBI, the Navy, and the State Department.[29]

8:55pm, LBJ Library, Austin, Texas.
25. *Lopez Report*, p.27.
26. *Ibid.*, pp.91–93.
27. *Ibid.*, p.18.
28. CIA employees: *ibid.*, pp.94–106. Louis Stokes: NARA RIF no. 180–10140–10175.
29. The reply from CIA headquarters: NARA RIF no. 104–10015–10048. For the

Not only were individuals within the CIA's headquarters and Mexico City office aware of Oswald's identity, but they were of course aware also of the significance of a US citizen making contact with communist officials. According to one of the CIA officers who helped to issue the cable from headquarters to Mexico City on 10 October, the reply revealed that the Agency possessed "a keen interest in Oswald on a need–to–know basis" just six weeks before President Kennedy's assassination. CIA headquarters obscured its "keen interest in Oswald" by withholding from the Mexico City station the fact that it was aware of certain incriminating activities which Oswald had undertaken in New Orleans a few weeks before his trip to Mexico City.[30]

The description of Lee Oswald sent by CIA headquarters to its Mexico City office on 10 October was not entirely accurate. Other descriptions of Oswald in official files, most of them going back several years before the assassination, were also inaccurate, but in different ways. In some files, his name is given as Lee Henry Oswald; in others he is said to have acquired Soviet citizenship. In this example it is Oswald's weight that is incorrect. On the day of his arrest, Oswald weighed 131 pounds, not 165.[31]

This collection of inaccurate files was generated by the CIA's internal counter–intelligence department, which hoped to identify moles within the CIA and the FBI by noting where particular items of incorrect information surfaced. Although the existence in official files of many knowingly inaccurate descriptions of Oswald is not sinister in itself, this is further proof that Oswald was being followed closely by elements within the US intelligence community long before the assassination. It may or may not be coincidental that the item of incorrect information sent on 10 October surfaced very soon after the assassination, twice. Within fifteen minutes of the shooting in Dealey Plaza, a bystander described the gunman to the Dallas police as a "slender white male about 30, 5 feet 10, 165." The description is unlikely to be genuine: the bystander would not

misleading information sent to other institutions, see Newman, *op. cit.*, pp.398–399.
30. See Jefferson Morley, 'What Jane Roman Said, part 3' at http://www.history-matters.com/essays/frameup/WhatJaneRomanSaid/WhatJaneRomanSaid_3.htm. For Oswald in New Orleans, see Chapter 9, The Career of Lee Harvey Oswald, p.71 below.
31. Oswald's weight is noted on his fingerprint card: CE 630 (*WCHE*, vol.17, p.285).

have been able to ascertain the gunman's height or weight merely by glimpsing the upper half of his body from the street below, and the most obvious and distinctive aspect of the gunman's appearance, his clothes, are not mentioned. One eye–witness, Howard Brennan, echoed part of the bystander's description: "a white man in his early 30's, slender, nice looking, slender and would weigh about 165 to 175 pounds." Brennan differed, however, by describing the gunman's clothes and not giving the man's height. The bystander was never identified.[32] The same description was given to a policeman at the scene of Officer J.D. Tippit's murder, again by an unidentified member of the public: "a white male about 5' 10", weighing 160 to 170 pounds . . . brown bushy hair."[33]

The impersonation of Lee Harvey Oswald in Mexico City could only have been organised by people with knowledge of the CIA's surveillance of the Soviet and Cuban diplomatic compounds; in other words, members of: the Soviet regime, or the Cuban regime, or the Mexican government, or the US security system. The destruction of evidence and the transmission of false evidence could only have been organised by people with inside access to the CIA station in Mexico City.

32. Inspector Herbert Sawyer's account of his encounter with the bystander: *WCHE*, vol.6, pp.321–323. Howard Brennan: *WCHE*, vol.19, p.470. For the case that Sawyer's bystander was not Brennan, see Simpich, *op. cit.*, chapter 6, available at http://www.maryferrell.org/wiki/index.php/Featured_State_Secret_Chapter6, esp. note 3.

33. Gerald Hill and the Tippit bystander: *WCHE*, vol.7, p.47.

8 Silvia Odio and León Oswald

A large community of anti–Castro Cuban refugees was living in Dallas in 1963. One of them, Silvia Odio, claimed that she was visited one evening in late September by three anti–Castro sympathisers: two Hispanic men and one American, who was introduced to her as 'León Oswald'.[1] The conversation was largely in Spanish, which the American did not appear to understand. One of the Hispanic men claimed to be a friend of her father, who was a political prisoner in Cuba. She was told that the group had arrived in Dallas from New Orleans, that they were about to go on a trip, and that 'León Oswald' might join the resistance movement in Cuba. Lee Harvey Oswald had been living in New Orleans during the summer of 1963, and was about to travel to Mexico City, where he would attempt to obtain a visa to visit Cuba.

The next day, one of the Hispanic men telephoned Odio and described 'León', the American, as: a former Marine; a crack marksman; someone who thought that President Kennedy should have been assassinated after the unsuccessful invasion of Cuba at the Bay of Pigs in 1961; and, in her words, "kind of nuts." When Silvia Odio saw the television coverage of the assassination, she immediately recognised Oswald as her American visitor. She had observed the American visitor at close range for about twenty minutes, and was convinced that the man was Lee Oswald.[2] An erroneous story emerged that Silvia Odio already knew Oswald because he had attended anti–Castro meetings in Dallas.[3] Although there is some

1. Silvia Odio's account: *WCHE*, vol.11, pp.377–399.
2. Silvia Odio's testimony: *HSCA Appendix*, vol.10, p.26.
3. CE 3108 (*WCHE*, vol.26, p.738).

evidence that he had indeed attended such meetings,[4] Odio herself denied that she knew Oswald.[5]

Silvia Odio's story was corroborated by several sources, and appeared to be reliable. Her sister, Annie, who was staying with Silvia at the time of the visit, saw the men and independently recognised Oswald when she saw him on television after the assassination.[6] Silvia had mentioned the episode to two people within a few days of the visit: to her father in a letter and to her psychiatrist, Dr Burton Einspruch, in conversation. A letter from Amador Odio refers to Silvia's letter and to an unknown Cuban who claimed to be his friend.[7] Dr Einspruch "recalled that she told him of the visit prior to the assassination," and considered her to be a reliable witness.[8] Silvia and Annie Odio were reluctant to publicise their stories, and the episode became known only by chance. Soon after the assassination, the third Odio sister, Sarita, mentioned to a friend of Silvia's, Lucille Connell, that Silvia had met Oswald. The FBI learned that another friend of Connell's had met Jack Ruby. The FBI eventually interviewed Connell, who told them about Odio's encounter with 'León Oswald'.[9] Even the Warren Commission accepted that Odio was a believable witness. Wesley Liebeler, who interviewed Odio for the Commission, stated that "a number of details in the woman's story coincided with facts she could not possibly have known."[10] The House Select Committee on Assassinations likewise found "that Silvia Odio's testimony was essentially credible."[11]

According to Odio, the meeting may have occurred on Wednesday 25 September, but was more likely to have occurred on Thursday 26 September.[12] Either way, there was a problem: both of

4. CD 205, p.646.
5. CE 3147 (*WCHE*, vol.26, p.837). See also Steve Bocham, 'Understanding Silvia Odio: What the LaFontaines Don't Tell You,' *Kennedy Assassination Chronicles*, vol.2, issue 2 (Summer 1996), pp.28–31.
6. FBI report of an interview with Annie Odio: CE 2907 (*WCHE*, vol.26, pp.362–363).
7. Silvia Odio's account of the correspondence: *WCHE*, vol.11, pp.383–384. Amador Odio's letter: *WCHE*, vol.20, pp.688–691.
8. Dr Einspruch: *HSCA Appendix*, vol.10, p.30.
9. Lucille Connell and the FBI: *HSCA Appendix*, vol.10, p.28.
10. Edward Epstein, *Inquest: the Warren Commission and the Establishment of Truth*, Viking Press, 1966, p.102.
11. *HSCA Appendix*, vol.10, p.31.
12. The date of the visit: CE 3147 (*WCHE*, vol.26, p.836).

these dates coincided with Oswald's Mexico City adventure. Oswald is presumed to have been in New Orleans on the morning of 25 September, when a cheque in his name was cashed. Oswald could not have obtained the cheque before 8am on the 25th.[13] The Warren Commission was aware that Oswald may in fact have begun his journey to Mexico on 24 September, the day before the cheque arrived in New Orleans, but did not attempt to resolve the problem.[14] Oswald is presumed to have arrived in Mexico City early on 27 September, when he registered at a hotel and made his first visits to the Soviet and Cuban diplomatic compounds.[15]

Oswald could not drive,[16] and had little money. The bus was the only suitably economical mode of transport that Oswald could have taken if he had travelled to Mexico without an associate. Just one itinerary fitted the available dates. It involved three separate bus journeys. The first bus left New Orleans shortly after mid–day on the 25th and arrived in Houston, 350 miles (560 km) away, very late the same day. The second bus left Houston early on the morning of the 26th, and arrived in Laredo on the Mexican border that afternoon. The third bus left Nuevo Laredo on the Mexican side of the border an hour or so later, and arrived in Mexico City shortly before 10am on the 27th. This itinerary was the one used in the Warren Commission's reconstruction of Oswald's bus journey.[17] Although Oswald appears to have crossed the border on the 26th,[18] the documentary evidence that he entered and left Mexico by bus is inconclusive and suspicious. One list of passengers for the return journey, provided by the Mexican government, had the name 'Oswld' [*sic*] added fraudulently.[19] There is some evidence that Oswald may have travelled by car, according to a memo from J. Edgar Hoover to the FBI's legal attaché in Mexico City: "Until we can prove Oswald was on a bus, the possibility will always ex-

13. CE 2131, pp. 3–4 (*WCHE*, vol.24, pp.716–717).
14. CE 3045, p.2 (*WCHE*, vol.26, p.596).
15. Guillermo Garcia Luna, the owner of the Hotel del Comercio, claimed that Oswald checked in between 10:00am and 11:00am on Friday 27 September 1963: CE 2121, p.54 (*WCHE*, vol.24, p.597).
16. Oswald began taking driving lessons a few weeks later: CE 425 (*WCHE*, vol.17, p.151) and *WCHE*, vol.2, p.514.
17. *WR*, p.731.
18. *Ibid.*, p.323.
19. CE 2121, pp.99–111 (*WCHE*, vol.24, pp.619–625).

ist that he left by automobile as indicated in Mexican immigration records."[20]

In order to arrive in Mexico City on the 27th, Oswald must have set off from New Orleans on the 25th. New Orleans, however, is more than 500 miles (800 km) by road from Dallas. Without assistance, Oswald could not have reached Dallas in time to visit Silvia Odio on the 25th and then travel the 240 miles to Houston in time to catch his bus. This created several uncomfortable options. Either the real Oswald was on a bus hundreds of miles away when Silvia Odio was introduced to 'León Oswald' in Dallas, or Oswald met Odio in Dallas and then travelled to Mexico City by some other means, which must have involved assistance from at least one accomplice. A third possibility is that Oswald did not visit Mexico City at all. The episode posed a similar problem to that of the impostor in Mexico City: either Oswald had associates or he was impersonated in Dallas as well as in Mexico City.

The Silvia Odio incident created huge difficulties for the Warren Commission and the FBI. After some urgent prompting as the *Warren Report* was about to go to press,[21] the FBI produced three men who, it alleged, were Odio's visitors. This allowed the Commission to explain away the problem as one of faulty identification.[22] But this story fell apart even before the *Warren Report* was published. All three men denied it, and the one who was supposed to have been 'León Oswald' had a cast–iron alibi.[23]

Apart from the question of whether or not Oswald was impersonated, the more sinister issue is the telephone call to Silvia Odio which planted specific information linking Oswald to the assassination, and which can only plausibly be interpreted in one way: that he was being set up, seven weeks in advance, to take the blame for the assassination.

20. FBI Oswald Mexico City File, 105–3702–5.
21. CE 3045 (*WCHE*, vol.26, p.595).
22. *WR*, p.324.
23. For a refutation of the Warren Commission's version, and a good general account of the problem, see *HSCA Appendix*, vol.10, pp.21–32.

9 The Career of Lee Harvey Oswald

One of the first matters to be considered by the Warren Commission was also one of the most sensitive: an allegation that Lee Harvey Oswald, the only official suspect in the assassination of President Kennedy, had been a paid undercover agent of the FBI or the CIA. J. Lee Rankin, the Warren Commission's General Counsel, was told in January 1964 by a reliable source that it was common knowledge among journalists in Texas that Oswald had regularly received $200 per month from the FBI.

Stories had already emerged that Soviet officials had met Oswald in Mexico City a few weeks before the assassination. These stories had generated competing conspiracy theories that blamed either the Soviets or the US security system for the killing. The Warren Commission was established specifically to counteract these conspiracy theories. If it became widely believed that Oswald had been secretly employed by a federal agency, the Commission would of course have found it almost impossible to make a convincing case that the alleged assassin had acted alone. Rankin and Earl Warren were determined to silence the rumours. The matter was discussed at an emergency meeting of the Commission on 22 January 1964. Two days later, Rankin and Warren met officials from Texas, who repeated the FBI rumour and mentioned other rumours about a connection between Oswald and the CIA. According to FBI interviews with one of the officials, Rankin swore them to secrecy. At the next meeting of the Warren Commission, on 27 January, Rankin discussed the FBI rumour but did not mention Oswald's alleged connection with the CIA. Secrecy was extended to the records of the various meetings. Part of the 22 January meeting took place off the record, and the stenographer's notes of the remainder of the meeting were destroyed. A tape recording survived only by chance. No stenographer was present at the 24 January meeting; the only record was a memo by Rankin.[1] These documents only came to light many years later, as the result of litigation under the Freedom of Information Act.

Some of the details of these rumours were almost certainly false. The FBI numbers attributed to Oswald, S172 or S179, did not follow the normal pattern for paid informants, which was: an abbreviation for the agent's local office (e.g. DL for Dallas, or NO for New Orleans) followed by an arbitrary four–digit number, and finally 'S' if the informant provided information on security–related matters, as Oswald was alleged to have done. Alonso Hudkins, the journalist at the centre of the affair, later claimed that he had invented the numbers. The CIA number, 110669, did follow that agency's normal pattern.[2] Some corroboration for the rumours appeared during the HSCA investigation in the late 1970s. William Walter, a member of the FBI's office in New Orleans, claimed that he had seen an FBI teletype which showed that Oswald had been an informant for that office. James Wilcott, a former CIA payroll officer, claimed that it was widely assumed among his CIA colleagues that Oswald had been a full–time employee of the Agency, although the HSCA was unable to find any support for this and "concluded that Wilcott's allegation was not worthy of belief."[3]

The rumours about Oswald's possible connections to the FBI and CIA were largely kept out of public view for many years. Other information became available soon after Oswald's arrest and murder which showed that he was not just an order–filler at a book warehouse. The more information that came to light, the more unusual his career appeared to be: he was a former Marine who had defected to the Soviet Union; he had been involved in both pro–

1. J. Lee Rankin's memo: CIA document 487–195A, Record Copy 201–0289248.
2. Secret Service interview with Hudkins: Secret Service Report 767, part of CD 320. FBI interviews with Hudkins and the Texas officials: FBI HQ Oswald File 105–82555–100. For a full discussion of this episode, see Gerald D. McKnight, *Breach of Trust: How the Warren Commission Failed the Nation and Why*, University Press of Kansas, 2005, pp.128–147.
3. William Walter: NARA RIF no. 180–10076–10413. James Wilcott: HSCA Interview of James B. Wilcott, 22 March 1978 and *HSCA Report*, pp.199–200.

and anti–Castro activity in New Orleans; and he had a strong interest in purchasing weapons by mail order.

Oswald was one of a series of former US military types who defected to the Soviet Union between 1958 and 1960. Some of this group of military defectors appear to have been compromised by the Soviets; others appear to have been working for US intelligence.[4] Oswald was armed with a very good knowledge of Russian, at least some of which he seems to have acquired at a specialist military language school, the Defense Language Institute in California. The Warren Commission appears to have heard, from sources not yet publicly identified, that Oswald had received instruction from the Defense Language Institute: "We are trying to run that down to find out what he studied at the Monterey School of the Army in the way of languages."[5] He had spent about three months at a Marine base not far from Monterey. According to the portion of his Marine Corps record that has been made public, Oswald had been tested in the Russian language while in the Marines, which implies that he had been taught Russian while in the Marines. Needless to say, foreign language tuition and testing were not normally part of Marine Corps life. Oswald had no significant knowledge of any other foreign language.[6]

Oswald's return to the USA in 1962 appeared to be actively condoned by the US authorities. Despite having promised to hand over state secrets to the Soviet regime, Oswald was not prosecuted. The State Department had assisted his return, by lending him the fare for the trans–Atlantic ocean crossing.[7] Oswald and his Russian wife settled in the Dallas area, where they were befriended by George de Mohrenschildt, a petroleum geologist with connections to US intelligence. They mixed socially with the strongly anti–Soviet Russian *émigré* community in Dallas.[8]

4. For military defectors, see John Newman, *Oswald and the CIA*, Carroll and Graf, 1995, pp.169–173 and 182–190. For an example of a US undercover agent in the Soviet Union, see NARA RIF no. 104–10066–10201, p.6.

5. Warren Commission Executive Session, 27 January 1964, p.192. For Oswald's knowledge of Russian in 1959, see CE 2015, p.8 (*WCHE*, vol.24, p.430) and Edward Epstein, *Inquest: the Warren Commission and the Establishment of Truth*, Viking Press, 1966, p.87.

6. Near Monterey: CD 113. Oswald's Marine Corps record: *WCHE*, vol.19, pp.656–768.

7. The loan from the State Department: *WR*, p.770.

8. George de Mohrenschildt's connections to the world of intelligence were origi-

Oswald applied for a new passport in June 1963, stating on the application form that he was planning to travel to the Soviet Union. The passport was granted the next day, an instance of bureaucratic efficiency that was noted during a meeting of the Warren Commission: "one of the strange things that happened, and it may have no bearing on this [the rumour that Oswald was an informer] at all, is the fact that this man who is a defector ... could walk about the Immigration Office in New Orleans one day and come out the next day with a passport that permitted him to go to Russia. From my observations of the case[s] that have come to us, such passports are not passed out with that ease."[9] An FBI memo made Oswald's status clear: "With Oswald's background we should have had a stop on his passport, particularly since we did not definitely know whether or not he had any intelligence assignments at that time."[10] Any intelligence assignments that justified the granting of a US passport must, of course, have been on behalf of US intelligence.

Lee Oswald moved to New Orleans in April 1963, ostensibly to find work. He made contact with several Cuban anti–Castro activists, including Carlos Bringuier, who was in charge of public relations for two organisations: the Cuban Revolutionary Council and the *Directorio Revolucionario Estudiantil*.[11] Oswald surprised Bringuier by offering to assist with a paramilitary training camp operated partly by the DRE. Bringuier declined the offer; he assumed that Oswald was an infiltrator working for either the pro–Castro movement or a US agency such as the FBI.[12] Bringuier's suspicions seemed to be justified when he encountered Oswald a few days later, distributing 'Hands Off Cuba!' leaflets on behalf

nally denied, but have since become better known. For his background, see *HSCA Appendix*, vol.12, pp.53–55.

9. Details of Oswald's passport application are summarised in this FBI report: CE 1062 (*WCHE*, vol.22, p.12). "Strange things": Warren Commission Executive Session, 22 January 1964, pp.7–8.

10. *HSCA Appendix*, vol.3, p.541.

11. For Oswald's links to anti–Castro Cubans in New Orleans, see Peter Dale Scott, *Deep Politics and the Death of JFK*, University of California Press, 1993, pp.80–92. The HSCA's assertion (*HSCA Appendix*, vol.10, p.62) that Bringuier was unconnected to the Cuban Revolutionary Council is false; see Scott, *op. cit.*, p.327 n.21.

12. Carlos Bringuier: *WCHE*, vol.10, p.35. For US intelligence activity in relation to both pro– and anti–Castro Cubans, see the *Schweiker–Hart Report*, pp.10–21. Although both the FBI as an agency and its senior officers as individuals were sympathetic to the anti–Castro movement, the Bureau also had to respond to pressure to limit the public's access to weapons.

of the Fair Play for Cuba Committee, a pro–Castro organisation specifically targetted by the DRE. The two men got into an argument, the police were called, and Oswald spent the night in jail. Oswald's release from jail was covered by the local news media.

Two more publicity stunts helped to identify him further with the pro–Castro cause. He hired assistants for a brief session of handing out FPCC leaflets. The session was covered on television; according to one of Oswald's assistants, the leafletting took no longer than 15 minutes, which suggests that the television station had been alerted in advance.[13] After being interviewed on a local radio station, Oswald was invited to take part in a radio debate on the Cuban question, in which he claimed that he was a Marxist and a member of the FPCC.[14] At one point in the debate, Oswald hinted that his communist sympathies may not have been genuine: "I worked in Russia. I was under the protection of the, that is to say, I was not under the protection of the American government."[15]

There were two main consequences of Oswald's activity. When applying for a Cuban visa in Mexico City a few weeks later, he made use of the pro–Castro credentials he had acquired in New Orleans. Within hours of the assassination, members of the DRE contacted several news organisations, supplying the evidence of the radio debate and pointing out the loyalty to the Castro regime of the apparent FPCC member and alleged assassin.[16] As a result, the FPCC was obliged to disband in December 1963. The FPCC had been a long–standing target of the FBI; according to an FBI memo from the time of Oswald's activities in New Orleans, "CIA is also giving some thought to planting deceptive information which might embarrass the [Fair Play for Cuba] Committee."[17]

13. Charles Steele, Jr: *WCHE*, vol.10, p.66.
14. A transcript of the interview: *WCHE*, vol.21, pp.621–632. A transcript of the debate: *ibid.*, pp.633–641. Recordings survive of the interview and the debate: http://www.maryferrell.org/wiki/index.php/Audio_-_Other.
15. Oswald's umming and ahhing has been omitted from this transcript. His apparent admission begins at about 15 minutes 45 seconds into the 23–minute programme. The official transcript incorrectly reads: "I worked in Russia. I was not under the protection of the — that is to say I was not under the protection of the American government." See *WCHE*, vol.21, p.639.
16. The DRE and the radio debate: *HSCA Appendix*, vol.10, pp.85–86.
17. The FBI and CIA against the FPCC: *Schweiker–Hart Report*, p.65; and Newman, *op. cit.*, pp.236–244.

A CIA document from several years later stated that the DRE was "an anti–Castro organization conceived, created, and funded by the CIA."[18] The DRE received $51,000 per month from the CIA through a propaganda operation directed by George Joannides. As the historian Gerald McKnight points out, "The unappreciated irony in this whole business was that the first JFK assassination conspiracy theory to find its way into print was paid for by George E. Joannides, a CIA psychological warfare specialist."[19] In his later role as the liaison officer between the CIA and the House Select Committee on Assassinations, Joannides ensured that the HSCA remained unaware of the Agency's financial and operational links to the DRE.[20]

Oswald's pro–Castro activity was not, however, what it seemed. Despite his left–wing media persona, Oswald had no known left–wing associates. The New Orleans branch of the FPCC consisted only of Oswald and one A.J. Hidell, which was presumed to be an alias for Oswald himself. Whether or not it actually was an alias, the name 'Hidell' functioned as an alias for Oswald. Both Oswald and Hidell were linked to the post office box to which the sixth–floor rifle was sent.[21] Oswald himself ensured that official records associated his name with Hidell and with sympathy for the Castro regime. In jail on the morning after the scuffle with Bringuier, Oswald requested, and was granted, an interview with an FBI agent, in which he produced a membership card which linked his and Hidell's names with the FPCC.[22] This information was duly relayed to the 112th Army Military Intelligence Group and the Office of Naval Intelligence, whose files surfaced immediately after the assassination.[23]

Some of Oswald's FPCC leaflets were stamped with an address, 544 Camp Street, which had no connection to the organisation. On

18. NARA RIF no. 104–10170–10156.
19. McKnight, *op. cit.*, p.350.
20. For more about the publication of Oswald's radio debate, and the relationship between the DRE and the CIA, see Jefferson Morley, 'What Jane Roman Said, part 6,' at http://www.history-matters.com/essays/frameup/WhatJaneRomanSaid/WhatJaneRomanSaid_6.htm.
21. The post office box: *WR*, pp.119–120.
22. The FPCC membership card: *WCHE*, vol.10, p.54; *WCHE*, vol.4, p.434.
23. 112th Military Intelligence Group linked Oswald and Hidell: *HSCA Report*, p.222. See also Scott, *op. cit.*, pp.84, 258–260.

the contrary, the building was associated with strongly anti–Castro interests. In 1962 it had been used as a base by the Cuban Revolutionary Council, and in 1963 it housed the offices of a private detective agency run by W. Guy Banister, a former FBI agent who was working at arms' length for the FBI and other federal agencies on a number of projects, including anti–Castro activity.[24] Oswald was a frequent visitor to Banister's office, according to several people who worked there, including Banister's secretary.[25] Banister, who was very much opposed to the FPCC and the Castro regime, also associated with Oswald in public. William Gaudet, a CIA asset who was peripherally involved in Oswald's Mexico City adventure, told the HSCA that "on one occasion be [*sic*] observed Oswald speaking to Guy Bannister [*sic*] on a street corner."[26] The historian Michael Kurtz, who was a student in New Orleans in 1963, saw the supposedly left–wing Oswald in the company of the undoubtedly right–wing Banister on two occasions, one of which involved Banister speaking at length to a group of students: "Bannister [*sic*] took what can only be called an extremist right–wing position, vehemently advocating a return to racial segregation, criticizing the students for attending an integrated university, and insisting that the United States launch a full–scale military invasion of Cuba." Kurtz concluded that "Oswald's public image as a pro–Castro Marxist was a façade masking the anti–Castro and anti–Communist agitator beneath."[27]

Guy Banister was not Lee Oswald's only curious associate in the summer of 1963. Antonio Veciana was the leader of Alpha 66,

24. For the Camp Street address on Oswald's literature, see CD 1495 and CE 3120 (*WCHE*, vol.26, p.783). For Banister's agency as a proxy or subcontractor for federal investigators, see *HSCA Appendix*, vol.10, p.130, and Scott, *op. cit.*, pp.86–90.
25. For Oswald's association with Banister and his anti–Castro activity, see: James DiEugenio, *Destiny Betrayed: JFK, Cuba and the Garrison Case*, 2nd edition, Skyhorse Publishing, 2012, pp.110–114; Anthony Summers, *Not In Your Lifetime: The Assassination of JFK*, Headline, 2013, pp.272–280; and Newman, *op. cit.*, pp.308–310.
26. For William Gaudet, see *HSCA Report*, pp.218–219 and Newman, *op. cit.*, pp.346–347. For Gaudet's Mexico City connection, see Scott, *op. cit.*, p.96 and notes 12–14 on pp.331–332.
27. Michael L. Kurtz, *Crime of the Century: The Kennedy Assassination from a Historian's Perspective*, 2nd edition, University of Tennessee Press, 1993, p.xxxix and p.204. See also Michael L. Kurtz, 'Lee Harvey Oswald in New Orleans: a Reappraisal,' *Louisiana History*, vol.21 no.1 (Winter 1980), pp.7–22, which discusses Oswald's involvement in Banister's pro–segregationist activity, although Kurtz often cites only "confidential interviews" as his sources.

one of the most aggressive groups of anti–Castro Cuban exiles. He claimed that on one occasion in late August or early September he turned up for an appointment with his CIA handler, who went under the assumed name of 'Maurice Bishop', and found 'Bishop' in the company of a young man whom Veciana recognised after the assassination as Lee Oswald. Veciana stated that "I am sure it was Oswald. If it wasn't Oswald, it was someone who looked exactly like him." Veciana later identified 'Maurice Bishop' as David Atlee Phillips, who in 1963 was based in Mexico City, where he ran the CIA's anti–Castro operations, including its subversion of the Fair Play for Cuba Committee. Phillips was the main source of the false claim that all recordings and photographs of Oswald in Mexico City had been routinely destroyed before the assassination.[28]

Oswald was very interested in purchasing weapons by mail order, both during the summer of 1963 in New Orleans and at the beginning of the year while living in Dallas. In addition to the rifle found on the sixth floor and the revolver found on Oswald when he was arrested, Dallas police discovered among his possessions several complete advertisements for weapons and at least five mail order coupons. One of these coupons, for a Mannlicher Carcano rifle from Klein's Sporting Goods of Chicago, was matched to a specific copy of the June 1963 issue of *American Rifleman* magazine which contained his thumb print.[29] This copy of the magazine was discovered by the FBI and the Secret Service on the day after the assassination, in a garage in New Orleans. In June 1963 Oswald had been working in a building next door to the garage. The proprietor of the garage claimed that Oswald had often spoken to him about guns, and in particular about how to obtain them by mail order.[30]

28. For Veciana's encounter with 'Maurice Bishop' and Oswald, see Gaeton Fonzi, *The Last Investigation*, Thunder's Mouth Press, 1993, pp.140–144; and Summers, *op. cit.*, pp.302–304. Veciana repeated his claims at a conference to mark the fiftieth anniversary of the publication of the *Warren Report*; see 'Skeptics gather 50 years after Warren Commission report about JFK assassination,' *Boston Globe*, 27 September 2014. For David Phillips and the FPCC, see Newman, *op. cit.*, p.241. For Phillips and the recordings, see Fonzi, *op. cit.*, p.285.
29. For Hidell's purchases, see *WR*, p.723, and Martha Moyer, 'Ordering the Rifle,' *Kennedy Assassination Chronicles*, vol.2 no.1 (March 1996), pp.23–31. For Oswald's thumb print, see CD 75, p.456, and Henry Hurt, *Reasonable Doubt: An Investigation into the Assassination of John F. Kennedy*, Henry Holt, 1985, p.298.
30. Oswald's conversations about guns: *WCHE*, vol.10, pp.220–227.

There seems to be no legitimate reason why Oswald should have wanted to order guns while in New Orleans. Several months earlier, a Mannlicher Carcano rifle of the same type as that found on the sixth floor of the Texas School Book Depository had been ordered and received by 'A. Hidell' from Klein's Sporting Goods of Chicago, using a coupon in the February 1963 issue of *American Rifleman*. Likewise, 'A.J. Hidell' had bought Oswald's revolver by mail order in January 1963.[31]

The *Warren Report* argued that Oswald "no doubt . . . purchased his weapons under the name of Hidell in an attempt to prevent their ownership from being traced,"[32] but failed to notice that the use of a pseudonym obscured his real identity only from the vendors. To those investigating the assassination, the name 'Hidell' was easily matched to Oswald through their use of the same post office box. The Commission also failed to notice that if Oswald had wished to obscure his identity fully, an almost foolproof method existed which he did not use. When the mysterious Mr Hidell had ordered the revolver and the rifle, Oswald was living in Dallas, Texas. The easiest way to obtain a weapon in Texas in 1963, and the only sensible way for an aspiring assassin, was to visit one of any number of shops which would sell one over the counter. No identification was needed, and no incriminating paper trail would exist. Identification was only required, and an incriminating paper trail created, when purchasing a weapon from a different state, by mail order.

In 1962 and 1963, the growing trade in mail–order weapons was being investigated by two official bodies: the Alcohol, Tobacco and Tax Division of the Internal Revenue Service, and a subcommittee of the Senate Judiciary Committee, headed by Senator Thomas Dodd.[33] Among the organisations under investigation were: the American Nazi Party, whose officials' names and addresses featured in Oswald's address book;[34] Cuban exile organisations, including three with whom Oswald had attempted to make contact in New Orleans and Dallas; Klein's Sporting Goods, of Chicago,

31. For the history of the weapons associated with Oswald, see *WR*, pp.118–121.
32. *WR*, p.315.
33. For the Dodd Committee's activities, which included the use of undercover investigators who purchased guns, see Hurt, *op. cit.*, pp.300–302.
34. Oswald's address book: CE 18 (*WCHE*, vol.16, pp.37–70).

from whom 'A. Hidell' had purchased by mail order a 36–inch–long Mannlicher Carcano rifle, the same model as the 40–inch–long rifle that was discovered on the sixth floor of the TSBD; and Seaport Traders, of Los Angeles, from whom 'A.J. Hidell' had purchased by mail order the revolver which was found on Oswald when he was arrested on 22 November 1963.

There is no categorical proof that Lee Oswald was working for one or another agency of the US government, either directly or through a proxy, but the circumstantial evidence is overwhelming. It is unclear whether Oswald himself, using the Hidell alias, purchased the 40–inch–long rifle which would link him directly to the assassination. A more important issue is also unclear: how much of Oswald's activity in New Orleans, Mexico City and Dallas was directed by others specifically in order to incriminate him, and how much of it was genuine undercover work that was seized on at some stage in the planning of the assassination. Several aspects of the Mexico City episode, for example, can be interpreted as an attempt by the counter–intelligence branch of the CIA to expose Soviet moles within the US security system. Oswald need not have been, and probably was not, a straightforward employee of one agency.

10 JFK Assassination Conspiracy Theories

Because the assassination of President Kennedy has not yet been properly investigated by the authorities, there is no widely accepted solution to the crime. Snippets of evidence point in many directions, and have helped to generate a large number of conspiracy theories, varying from the plausible to the outlandish.

The first conspiracy theories appeared almost at once, prompted by information in the earliest news reports, and were amplified over the next few days. Evidence of Lee Harvey Oswald's defection to the Soviet Union, and his apparent sympathy with the Cuban regime, helped to generate the earliest theories, which claimed that he had been working for the Cubans or Soviets, either as a lone gunman or with associates. The communist conspiracy theory was inflamed a few days after the assassination by a report from Mexico that Oswald had accepted $6,500 from a representative of the Cuban regime as an advance payment for killing Kennedy, although the report was soon shown to be false. The supposed encounter took place in Mexico City on 18 September 1963, when Oswald was known to have been in New Orleans.[1]

The notion of an international communist conspiracy had been used as a propaganda tool to contain political dissent in the US for many years before the assassination. Its application to this case turned out to be tenuous, partly because of the suspicion that Oswald's communist sympathies were not genuine, and partly because it was difficult to imagine any plausible reasons why the

1. For Gilberto Alvarado's claim, see Peter Dale Scott, *Deep Politics and the Death of JFK*, University of California Press, 1993, pp.121–124, and *WR*, p.307.

Soviet regime might have wanted to replace President Kennedy with the less predictable Lyndon Johnson. Any credible evidence that the Soviets were behind the assassination would have risked precipitating a nuclear war, which had only narrowly been averted during the Cuban missile crisis just one year earlier. There is no good reason to believe that Oswald had been co–opted by the Soviet regime. Yuri Nosenko, a KGB officer who defected to the USA in 1964, claimed that Oswald had not been recruited by the KGB, either before or after his defection. Although senior officials within the US intelligence system disbelieved Nosenko, his claims were corroborated by the KGB's files on Oswald, which were made public in 1999.[2]

The Castro regime, on the other hand, seemed to possess a plausible motive for sponsoring the assassination. In 1959, a few months after a nationalist revolution had overthrown the US client regime in Cuba, President Eisenhower authorised military attacks against the island, and in 1960 he authorised a series of assassination attempts against Fidel Castro himself. Eisenhower's policy continued under President Kennedy, who escalated the military attacks. One assassination plot against Castro was actually in progress on the day of Kennedy's own assassination, involving CIA agents and a former Castro loyalist, Rolando Cubela Secades, code–named AM/LASH.[3] One theory has it that Castro, who was well aware of the plots, took revenge by turning a set of assassins back on Kennedy. In the words of the historian Michael Kurtz:

> I believe that Fidel Castro ordered the assassination of President Kennedy in retaliation for the repeated assassination attempts against his own life during the Kennedy administration. To repeat what Lyndon Johnson told Howard K. Smith and Joseph A. Califano, "Kennedy was trying to get Castro, but Castro got him first."[4]

2. The KGB's Oswald files, in Russian with an English translation: http://www.paperlessarchives.com/FreeTitles/OswaldKGB.pdf (PDF: 9.2 MB).
3. For the assassination attempts on Castro, see the CIA Inspector General's *Report on Plots to Assassinate Fidel Castro*, 1967, NARA RIF no. 104–10213–10101. For Kennedy's approval of the plots, see Church Committee Interim Report: *Assassination Plots Involving Foreign Leaders*, US Government Printing Office, 1975, p.141.
4. Michael Kurtz, *Crime of the Century, The Kennedy Assassination from a Historian's Perspective*, 2nd edition, University of Tennessee Press, 1993, pp.xlvi–xlvii.

Castro's motive would have been straightforward: personal survival. If he had expected the assassination attempts against him to continue indefinitely, the risk of provoking another military invasion might have been worth taking. There are, however, good reasons to doubt Fidel Castro's involvement in the JFK assassination. The strongest evidence linking the Cuban regime with the assassination is the dubious pro–Castro affiliation of the only person officially associated with the crime. Like the Soviets, Castro would not have expected his treatment to improve under Johnson. There was no reason for Castro to presume that the CIA's attacks would continue indefinitely under Kennedy; he was aware that President Kennedy was attempting from late September 1963 to mend relations between the Cuban and US regimes.[5]

The early communist conspiracy theory quickly prompted a second theory. The blatant evidence of Cuban and Soviet involvement was taken to be a fraudulent attempt by their political opponents to blame those regimes. Both theories generated public distrust of established political institutions. This in turn led directly to the establishment of the Warren Commission, which had been given ten months, a staff of 70, and huge financial and legal powers, and was expected to come up with convincing evidence that Lee Harvey Oswald was the lone assassin of President Kennedy. When the weakness of the *Warren Report*'s case against Oswald became widely known, the way was open for conspiracy theories to fill the explanatory gap. The majority of the post–Warren Commission theories named a variety of establishment and right–wing suspects. Not every theory focussed exclusively on one set of suspects; many theorists filled their plates with helpings from several areas of the conspiracy buffet.

One crucial factor set a barrier that few of these conspiracy theories were able to overcome. It was clear that whether or not Oswald had been aware of the assassination plot in advance, he had been carefully set up to take the blame. The Silvia Odio incident shows that the framing of Oswald was an integral part of the assassination of President Kennedy. Oswald's undercover work shows

5. For an account of the covert meetings between representatives of Kennedy and Castro in the two months immediately before the assassination, see James Douglass, *JFK and the Unspeakable: Why He Died and Why It Matters*, Orbis Books, 2008, pp.69–74, 248–50.

that he was being directed by one or more US intelligence organisations. Oswald's impersonation in Mexico City shows that his framing was facilitated, whether knowingly or otherwise, by elements within the CIA. We can therefore rule out as a prime mover in the assassination any individual or organisation that did not possess two things: knowledge of Oswald's undercover activities, and access to the workings of the CIA's office in Mexico City. Several of the most popular suspects probably knew nothing of Oswald's undercover work, and certainly could not have had access to the CIA's Mexico City office.

Lyndon Johnson was the most obvious direct beneficiary of the assassination. He certainly possessed the motive. There had been rumours that Kennedy had been planning to replace Johnson as vice–presidential candidate in the 1964 election. Johnson's political career was being threatened by a corruption scandal, which his accession to the presidency allowed him to overcome. There is, however, no convincing evidence that he had any advance knowledge of the assassination. One especially ludicrous version of the LBJ conspiracy theory claimed that Johnson attended a party on the evening before the assassination, at which he announced to a room full of senior politicians and Texan oil millionaires that the president was to be killed the next day.[6]

Kennedy and J. Edgar Hoover did not get on, but that is hardly a credible reason for one to kill the other. The FBI was not under any threat from the Kennedy administration. Hoover's only plausible motive was that he may have feared that Kennedy would force him out of office when he reached the mandatory retirement age of 70 in 1965. The FBI's eagerness to seize control of the investigation, and its lack of willingness to investigate the assassination fully, do not imply that it or its director were involved in the crime. Institutional reasons are sufficient to explain its role in the cover–up. The impersonation of Oswald in Mexico City, coupled with the widespread public suspicion that a conspiracy had occurred, demanded the adoption of the politically harmless lone–

6. The 'LBJ did it' theory was first put forward in print by Joachim Joesten, *The Dark Side of Lyndon Baines Johnson*, Peter Dawn Ltd, 1968. For the announcement at the party, see Madeleine Brown, *Texas in the Morning*, Conservatory Press, 1997. For examples of Johnson's legendary corruption, see Clark R. Mollenhoff, *Despoilers of Democracy*, Doubleday, 1965.

nut theory. Lee Oswald's association with the former FBI agent Guy Banister in New Orleans, and the rumours that Oswald had been an informer for the FBI, obliged the Bureau to conceal any links it might have had to the alleged assassin.[7]

The Secret Service was in charge of the president's security, and clearly failed in its job. It was largely responsible for setting the route of the motorcade and for ensuring that the buildings along the route were secure. While the Secret Service as an institution had neither a credible motive nor the ability to carry out the assassination by itself, it is not inconceivable that one or more members of the Secret Service facilitated the assassination, although there is no serious evidence to support the idea. The Secret Service seems to have attracted some of the most implausible JFK assassination conspiracy theories, such as the notion that Kennedy's driver, a Secret Service agent, fired the fatal shot. Sadly for the theory, the Zapruder film shows clearly that William Greer, the driver, was holding nothing more dangerous than the steering wheel, and that the fatal shot hit Kennedy on the right side of his head while Greer was sitting to the president's left. Another theory claimed that the Zapruder film was altered to conceal the driver's complicity in bringing the car to a halt just before the fatal head shot. An equally absurd non–conspiracy theory claimed that a Secret Service agent in the car behind Kennedy fired the fatal shot by accident. This theory was heavily promoted by the media at the time of the fiftieth anniversary, despite having been debunked on its first outing twenty years earlier. Charles Bronson's home movie of the assassination shows that the agent, George Hickey, was not pointing his gun at anyone. Hickey sued the author and publisher who first promoted the theory, and was reported to have received an out–of–court payment.[8]

7. Mark North, *Act of Treason: The Role of J. Edgar Hoover in the Assassination of President Kennedy*, Skyhorse Publishing, 1991, argues for Hoover's involvement.
8. For the 'Secret Service driver shot Kennedy' theory, see Dan Robertson, *Definitive Proof: The Secret Service Murder of President John Fitzgerald Kennedy*, Lulu.com, 2006. For the Zapruder film hoax theory, see Appendix D, Is the Zapruder Film Authentic?, p.161 below. For the accidental shooting theory, see Bonar Menninger, *Mortal Error: The Shot That Killed JFK*, St. Martin's Press, 1992; and Michael James, 'Lawsuit is settled in favor of former Secret Service agent; book claimed man accidentally fired bullet that killed Kennedy,' *Baltimore Sun*, 3 February 1998. Details of Hickey's legal claim are available at http://mcadams.posc.mu.edu/complaint.txt.

A majority of anti–Castro Cubans considered US policy on Cuba to be insufficiently aggressive. Many blamed Kennedy for the failure of the invasion of Cuba at the Bay of Pigs in 1961. Oswald's links to anti–Castro Cubans in New Orleans in the summer of 1963 suggest that if he had been involved in the planning of the assassination, perhaps they had too. If elements of the anti–Castro movement were behind the assassination, their actions had no practical effect. There was no significant difference between President Johnson's Cuban policies and Kennedy's.

Kennedy was very unpopular with racists and fascists, who took exception to his proposed civil rights legislation and to what they considered to be his failure to stand up to the communist menace. One such extremist, Joseph Milteer, appeared to have predicted two weeks before the assassination that Kennedy would be shot "from an office building with a high–powered rifle . . . they will pick up somebody within hours afterwards . . . just to throw the public off."[9] General Edwin Walker, whom Oswald was supposed to have attempted to kill in April 1963, was alleged to have been the fascist mastermind behind the conspiracy. Walker possessed both ideological and personal reasons for resenting Kennedy. He was an active member of the John Birch Society, which had been set up in 1958 by a group of business–owners to promote their authoritarian views and interests. Walker had been relieved of his command by Kennedy's Secretary of Defense, Robert McNamara, after indoctrinating his troops with John Birch Society propaganda. Following his participation in the violent protests against the enrolment of the first non–white student at the University of Mississippi in September 1962, Walker was ordered by the Attorney General, Robert Kennedy, to be committed to a mental institution.[10] Individuals sympathetic to the John Birch Society paid for an advertisement in the *Dallas Morning News* on 22 November 1963, lamenting what they saw as Kennedy's tolerance of communism at home and abroad. Others distributed leaflets accusing the president of trea-

9. Joseph Milteer: *HSCA Appendix*, vol.3, pp.447–450. See also a book by the FBI agent who dealt with Milteer and who took his claims seriously: Don Adams, *From an Office Building with a High–Powered Rifle*, Trine Day, 2012. The Secret Service was informed of the threat, but does not appear to have done anything about it; the Secret Service's account, Commission Document 3, does not mention it.

10. For the case that General Edwin Walker was involved in the JFK assassination, see W.R. Morris, *The Men Behind the Guns*, Angel Lea Books, 1975.

son, citing his "support and encouragement to the Communist inspired racial riots."[11] It is conceivable that people associated with extreme right–wing groups may have had advance knowledge of the assassination, but there is no solid evidence linking any such group to the shooting. Although Joseph Milteer boasted of his knowledge that Kennedy would be killed in Dallas, and implied that people sharing his views had played an active role, others placed the blame instead on their favourite enemy. Fred Koch, one of the wealthy businessmen who had founded the John Birch Society, and who in 1961 had published a pamphlet claiming that Earl Warren, Dwight Eisenhower and other prominent Americans were communist stooges, sponsored an advertisement in the *New York Times* after the assassination, alleging that Oswald had been part of a communist conspiracy.[12] The John Birch Society still exists; its website claims that "history is rarely accidental" but is keen to deny that the Society "played a role in the assassination of President Kennedy."[13]

The shooting of Oswald by Jack Ruby, two days after the shooting of Kennedy, was widely interpreted as the silencing of a potentially troublesome patsy. Rumours quickly spread about Ruby's connections to organised crime in Dallas and Chicago, his history of gun–smuggling, his links to the Dallas police, and his stalking of Oswald in the two days before the murder. Ruby's underworld connections were minimised by the Warren Commission, partly as a result of the failure of the FBI to supply the Commission with pertinent evidence, and partly because of the political necessity to portray Ruby, like Oswald, as a lone nut:

> [T]he Commission believes that the evidence does not

11. The text of the 'Welcome to Dallas' advertisement is online at http://www.latinamericanstudies.org/mrkennedy.htm. The 'Wanted for Treason' leaflet: http://commons.wikimedia.org/wiki/File:Wanted_for_treason.jpg.
12. The text of the advertisement blaming a communist conspiracy is online at http://mcadams.posc.mu.edu/birch.htm. For Fred Koch's beliefs and activities, see Yasha Levine, 'A People's History of Koch Industries: How Stalin Funded the Tea Party Movement,' at http://exiledonline.com/a-peoples-history-of-koch-industries-how-stalin-funded-the-tea-party-movement/; and Daniel Schulman, *Sons of Wichita: How the Koch Brothers Became America's Most Powerful and Private Dynasty*, Grand Central Publishing, 2014.
13. For the John Birch Society's current conspiratorial thinking, see http://www.jbs.org/issues-pages/conspiracy. Its denial of involvement in the JFK assassination: http://www.jbs.org/about-jbs/myths-vs-facts.

> establish a significant link between Ruby and organized crime. Both State and Federal officials have indicated that Ruby was not affiliated with organized criminal activity. And numerous persons have reported that Ruby was not connected with such activity.[14]

The House Select Committee on Assassinations compiled a 1000–page report on Ruby and concluded that, on the contrary, Jack Ruby "had a significant number of associations and direct and indirect contacts with underworld figures, a number of whom were connected to the most powerful La Cosa Nostra leaders. Additionally, Ruby had numerous associations with the Dallas criminal element."[15]

Peter Dale Scott points out that the HSCA too gave an incomplete account of Jack Ruby's activities that may have been relevant to the assassination:

> The Committee studiously avoided the following important propositions:
>
> - From as early as 1946–47, Ruby was involved in major narcotics dealings; and yet he was protected from arrest, most probably because he was also a US government informant.
> - Ruby was, as reported, involved in payoffs to the Dallas police, for whom he was unquestionably a narcotics informant.
> - Ruby was on good, but probably illicit, terms with judges and other high members of the Dallas political establishment.
> - According to his lawyer, Ruby was an informant for the Kefauver Committee [which investigated organised crime]; and in exchange for this service, the Kefauver Committee agreed to ignore contemporary organized crime and police corruption in

14. *WR*, p.801.
15. *HSCA Report*, p.149. For more about Ruby's background, see *HSCA Appendix*, vol.9, pp.125–1117, and Scott, *op. cit.*, pp.127–208. For the Dallas police's complicity in Ruby's murder of Oswald, see *HSCA Report*, pp.156–158.

Dallas, specifically with respect to the 1946 takeover by organized crime of the national racing wire service.

- The wire–service operation was a key organizing force for criminal activity in that era, including narcotics. Profits from the resulting system of protected crime (in which Ruby was somehow implicated) were invested in legitimate businesses (such as international hotels and defense industries like General Dynamics) which formed part of the expansive postwar US military–industrial establishment.

To sum up, the Warren Commission ... suppressed Ruby's links to organized crime and the political establishment. The House Committee rectified the first half of this suppression, but not the second.[16]

The mafia's close links to Jack Ruby suggest that it was involved at some level in the elimination of Oswald. The suspicion that the mafia was involved also in the assassination of Kennedy gained support in the 1970s, when it became known that the CIA had co–opted the services of senior mobsters for its assassination attempts on Fidel Castro. FBI wiretaps and informers revealed that several senior mafia figures expressed hatred toward the Kennedy brothers, who had forced the FBI and other agencies to take action against mobsters.[17]

The House Select Committee on Assassinations lent credence to the 'mafia killed JFK' theory. It concluded that although "organized crime, as a group, was not involved in the assassination ... individual members may have been involved."[18] The theory was stated more forcefully in a book by two prominent members of the HSCA, its chief counsel, Robert Blakey, and the editor of the *HSCA Report*, Richard Billings:

16. Scott, *op. cit.*, p.70.
17. For the mafia's attitude to the Kennedys, and for a representative sample of the 'mafia did it' theory, see David Scheim, *Contract on America: The Mafia Murder of President John F. Kennedy*, Zebra, 1989.
18. *HSCA Report*, p.147.

> [Ruby's] business activities were an integral part of a system of criminal operations, even if they were not illegal as such. At least on his trip to Cuba, Ruby played an important, if minor, role in a sophisticated syndicate operation that involved one of the most powerful underworld leaders. Ruby's associates in Dallas for the years and months prior to the assassination included a number of prominent organized–crime figures. He was in serious financial difficulty in the period leading up to the assassination, and a number of organized–crime figures were aware of it. Those same figures, under heavy pressure from the Kennedy organized–crime program, had a strong motive to assassinate the President....
>
> The murder of Oswald by Jack Ruby had all the hallmarks of an organized crime hit, an action to silence the assassin, so he could not reveal the conspiracy.[19]

The HSCA found both the FBI and the CIA to be at fault for the Warren Commission's inadequate treatment of Jack Ruby and the mafia:

> The committee concluded that the FBI's investigation into a conspiracy was deficient in the areas that the committee decided were most worthy of suspicion — organized crime, pro– and anti–Castro Cubans, and the possible associations of individuals from these areas with Lee Harvey Oswald and Jack Ruby. In those areas in particular, the committee found that the FBI's investigation was in all likelihood insufficient to have uncovered a conspiracy.[20]

> Virtually all former Warren Commission members and staff contacted by the committee said they regarded the CIA–Mafia plots against Fidel Castro to be the most important information withheld from the Commission. They all agreed that an awareness of the plots would

19. Robert Blakey and Richard Billings, *The Plot to Kill the President*, NYT Books, 1981, pp.338–339.
20. *HSCA Report*, p.242.

> have led to significant new areas of investigation and would have altered the general approach of the investigation. J. Lee Rankin, who was the Commission's General Counsel, said he was outraged on learning in 1975 of the CIA's use of underworld figures for Castro assassination plots.[21]

Not every member of the Warren Commission shared Rankin's ignorance or outrage. Allen Dulles had been director of the CIA under Eisenhower in 1960, when the Agency began using mobsters in its Castro assassination plots, and remained so until he was relieved of his duties by President Kennedy after the Bay of Pigs invasion. Dulles, who was the busiest member of the Commission after Earl Warren, evidently did not feel the need to enlighten his colleagues about the activities of his former employers.

No doubt the mafia could have performed the assassination, but they alone, like LBJ, the FBI, the Secret Service, pro– and anti–Castro Cubans, and assorted fascists, could not have framed Lee Oswald.

If there is one category of historical event in which conspiracy is not uncommon, it is the assassination of political figures. The idea that President Kennedy was killed as the result of a conspiracy is no more absurd than the idea that Julius Caesar, or Abraham Lincoln, or Archduke Franz Ferdinand, or Anwar Sadat, or Indira Gandhi, or any number of other prominent political figures were killed as the result of conspiracies. There is, however, one important difference between the JFK assassination and other, perfectly uncontroversial instances of conspiratorial assassinations. To claim that Julius Caesar, for example, was the victim of a political conspiracy does not threaten to diminish popular support for, or at least tolerance of, contemporary political institutions. Professional historians and commentators in the media, who instinctively defend such institutions, tend not to report the JFK assassination with the same objectivity that they usually apply to the assassinations of other historical figures.[22]

21. *Ibid.*, p.258.
22. Standard interpretations of Julius Caesar's life and death are not, however, entirely free from modern ideological considerations; see Michael Parenti, *The Assassination of Julius Caesar: A People's History of Ancient Rome*, The New Press, 2003.

Perhaps the most common explanation by the media for the existence of JFK assassination conspiracy theories is that people are unable to accept the notion that a great hero could be slain by a maladjusted loser. This is a reflection of the media's own representation of Kennedy in particular and the institution of the presidency in general. It is a poor explanation in two ways. Firstly, the historical record shows that conspiracy theories arose very quickly after the assassination and were based on reliable facts supplied by the media: the evidence of shots from the front, Oswald's contacts with Soviets and Cubans, and his convenient execution by Jack Ruby. Secondly, if JFK conspiracy theories are a reflection of any commonly held ideas, those ideas are more likely to be a general suspicion of US nation–state institutions rather than adoration of one of the state's figureheads. The media's flawed depiction of presidents as hero figures, deciding policy for high–minded reasons and with little interference from social institutions, is not unlike the conception of the world put forward by some conspiracy theorists. Political events happen for reasons of power, not principle. The media, like the more naive or paranoid conspiracy theorists, gives little consideration to the wider political context of the JFK assassination.

11 The Political Context of the JFK Assassination

President Kennedy's assassination has generated innumerable conspiracy theories, many of which fail to demonstrate a plausible relation between the assassination and Kennedy's role within the political system.

The CIA's reputation as a general-purpose bad guy ensures that it features heavily in many politically inspired conspiracy theories. Individuals within the agency certainly played a role in the JFK assassination, though perhaps unwittingly. In New Orleans, Oswald had performed what appears to have been an elaborate pantomime with a group funded by the CIA. The impersonation of Oswald in Mexico City, which had the effect of incriminating him after the assassination, cannot plausibly have been carried out without the participation of some members of the CIA.

The question of an institutional motive is less clear. There was animosity from senior CIA officers toward Kennedy, who had transferred some of the CIA's powers to the military in response to the Agency's behaviour during the failed invasion of Cuba at the Bay of Pigs, but this alone is hardly a convincing motive for the president's assassination.[1] The central role of certain members of the CIA in the framing of Oswald does not imply that the Agency as a whole had any involvement in the assassination. Such a notion is highly implausible, given that the CIA as an organisation almost

1. For the 'CIA killed JFK' theory, see e.g. Michael Calder, *JFK vs CIA: The Central Intelligence Agency's Assassination of the President*, West LA Publishers, 1998; and L. Fletcher Prouty, *JFK: The CIA, Vietnam and the Plot to Assassinate John F. Kennedy*, Citadel Press, 2003.

never acted contrary to policy laid down by the White House. One of the CIA's essential functions has been to carry out, and if necessary take the blame for, those aspects of official policy which the electorate could not be trusted to ratify, such as direct interference in the affairs of foreign regimes.[2]

Two exceptions to this rule involved aspects of Operation Mongoose, the CIA's terrorist campaign against the Castro regime and the general population of Cuba: the CIA's alliance with mobsters to carry out assassination attempts on Castro, in contravention of official anti–mafia policy, and its indulgence of the more enthusiastic anti–Castro Cubans in their military attacks on Cuban towns and ships at the same time as the White House was exploring ways to mend relations with Castro.[3] Although Operation Mongoose had been authorised by Kennedy, both examples contradicted the Kennedy administration's official policy at the time of the assassination, and each is pertinent to the assassination. The CIA, which helped to frame Oswald, was closely associated with elements of the mafia and the anti–Castro Cuban exile movement. It is not at all implausible that the assassination arose from within this loose alliance of interests.

The so–called military–industrial complex reflected the interests of domestic elites far more powerful than any *ad hoc* grouping of mobsters, anti–Castro Cubans, disaffected CIA agents and a few gung–ho generals who opposed President Kennedy's actions during the Cuban missile crisis. Oliver Stone's movie, *JFK*, popularised the notion that economic and military elites within the United States instigated President Kennedy's assassination largely because he was threatening to withdraw US military and financial support for its client regime in South Vietnam, with the consequences that: the military would not get their war; the owners of armaments and construction companies would not get their state–subsidised profits; and capitalist ideologues would lose their in-

2. The CIA carried out policy determined by the National Security Council, which was heavily influenced by the White House. For plausible deniability, the function that allows government officials to pass blame to the CIA, see the Church Committee Interim Report: *Assassination Plots Involving Foreign Leaders*, US Government Printing Office, 1975, pp.11–12.

3. The CIA's associations with mobsters was made public by the *Schweiker–Hart Report*. For the assassination attempts on Castro, see the CIA Inspector General's *Report on Plots to Assassinate Fidel Castro*, 1967, NARA RIF no. 104–10213–10101.

fluence over the economies of south–east Asia, with the possibility of a contagious outbreak of independent development throughout the US's sphere of influence.

There are two ways to interpret Kennedy's assassination and his relations with elite institutions: either he was working against the interests of established power, and was eliminated for institutional reasons, or he was working within the limits set by established power, and was eliminated by individuals or groups for reasons that had nothing to do with the interests of elite institutions. The first option defines the JFK assassination as a *coup d'état*; the second as a conspiracy. Although the wider definition of 'conspiracy' encompasses almost every *coup d'état*, a narrower definition is valuable in this case. Any worthwhile account of a political event must acknowledge the fundamental distinction between an action that is part of the normal functioning of established institutions and an action that is independent of such institutions. Many interpretations of the JFK assassination fail to make this distinction, which is crucial to any useful explanation of who killed Kennedy or why he was assassinated. The distinction is crucial also to understanding the significance of the assassination. The further removed any conspirators were from the institutions of power, the less the assassination has to tell us about the workings of the US political system.

The lack of a substantial change in official policy toward Cuba after the JFK assassination leaves only one credible reason why domestic elites might have had Kennedy removed from office by force: their disapproval of his policy toward Vietnam. Under the Kennedy administration, however, US financial and military support for the government in South Vietnam increased significantly, and the organised resistance of the South Vietnamese peasantry continued to be strongly suppressed. When Kennedy became president, there were about 700 members of the US military in South Vietnam; by November 1963, there were 16,700. The South Vietnamese army became larger and better equipped. A concentration camp system, known as the 'strategic hamlet program,' was established to contain dissent in rural areas. Chemical warfare was used in South Vietnam to destroy forests and crops, and napalm was used against rural villages. The US supported terrorist raids by South Vietnamese special forces in North Vietnam.[4]

One dominant theme is visible in the historical record of US policy discussions under the Kennedy administration: that the US military would withdraw from South Vietnam when the local regime had imposed its control over the population. In response to the changing military and political situation in South Vietnam, there was much debate in US military, diplomatic and political circles about the best way to achieve this end. President Kennedy began to favour a reduced role for the US military. On 11 October 1963, he signed National Security Action Memorandum no.263, which supported a proposal that the South Vietnamese army be trained to take over the essential elements of the US military's role, with the aim of allowing the US to withdraw 1,000 troops by the end of the year.[5]

This policy had first been proposed in April 1963, and was implemented in October when the corruption and harshness of Ngo Dinh Diem's regime were seen as counterproductive to US interests. The State Department interpreted the memorandum as a hint that the regime ought to ease its repression of dissidents and other political enemies. High–level discussions had been taking place for some time about whether or not to support a *coup* by a group of South Vietnamese generals against Diem. NSAM 263 failed to have the desired effect, and US officials approved a *coup*, which took place on 1 November. The following day, Diem and his brother, Ngo Dinh Nhu, were executed.[6] The *coup* was followed by more internal disruption. Three weeks later, official policy was redefined in another document, NSAM 273, which mentioned the

4. For US involvement in Vietnam under Kennedy, see Noam Chomsky, *Rethinking Camelot: JFK, the Vietnam War, and US Political Culture*, South End Press, 1993; and William Conrad Gibbons, ed., *The US Government and the Vietnam War: Executive and Legislative Roles and Relationships, Part 2 (1961–64)*, Princeton University Press, 1986, pp.70–71. The destruction of crops: *Foreign Relations of the United States, 1961–1963*, vol.2, US Government Printing Office, 1997, pp.673–675; and William A. Buckingham, *Operation Ranch Hand: The Air Force and Herbicides in Southeast Asia*, US Government Printing Office, 1982. The strategic hamlet program: Milton E. Osborne, *Strategic Hamlets in South Vietnam: A Survey and a Comparison*, Cornell University Southeast Asia Program Publications, 1970.

5. NSAM 263: *Foreign Relations of the United States, 1961–1963*, vol.4, US Government Printing Office, 1997, pp.395–396.

6. For US involvement in the *coup d'état* against Diem three weeks before the JFK assassination, see John Prados, 'JFK and the Diem Coup,' at http://www2.gwu.edu/~nsarchiv/NSAEBB/NSAEBB101/.

withdrawal of troops only in a general way as part of US "objectives," and proposed that US military involvement be extended to North Vietnam. The memorandum was drawn up the day before the JFK assassination, while Kennedy was in Texas, and was signed by Lyndon Johnson on 26 November.[7]

Johnson was more willing than Kennedy to be persuaded of the need to increase US military involvement in south–east Asia, but this does not imply that he was installed for that purpose, nor that it was necessary for Kennedy to be replaced in order for military involvement to increase. The first substantial increase under Johnson did not happen until February 1965. President Kennedy had consistently aligned himself with the less militaristic of his advisers, while remaining within the scope of acceptable debate. Although the official written record is incomplete, there is nothing in the publicly available documents to suggest that Kennedy strayed from the doctrine that the US military would only withdraw once the domestic rebellion was contained. Even if NSAM 263 had been interpreted by domestic elites as recommending unconditional military withdrawal, it could hardly have provoked Kennedy's assassination, the plans for which were clearly underway when Oswald or an impostor were seen in Mexico City and Dallas, two weeks before the memorandum was signed.[8]

In the speech he gave in Forth Worth a few hours before his assassination, Kennedy boasted of his loyalty to US elite institutions:

> In the past 3 years we have increased the defense budget of the United States by over 20 percent; increased the program of acquisition for Polaris submarines from 24 to 41; increased our Minuteman missile purchase program by more than 75 percent; doubled the number of strategic bombers and missiles on alert; doubled

7. NSAM 273: *Foreign Relations of the United States, 1961–1963*, vol.4, US Government Printing Office, 1997, pp.637–640. The extension of the war to North Vietnam is mentioned in paragraph seven.

8. For the case that President Kennedy's proposed withdrawal from Vietnam signified a drastic change in policy, see e.g. John Newman, *JFK and Vietnam: Deception, Intrigue, and the Struggle for Power*, Warner Books, 1992; Peter Dale Scott, *Deep Politics and the Death of JFK*, University of California Press, 1993, pp.24–37; and James K. Galbraith, 'Exit Strategy,' *Boston Review*, October–November 2003. For the case against, see e.g. Chomsky, *op. cit.*; and Richard J. Walton, *Cold War and Counter–Revolution: The Foreign Policy of John F. Kennedy*, Viking Press, 1972.

> the number of nuclear weapons available in the strategic alert forces; increased the tactical nuclear forces deployed in Western Europe by over 60 percent; added five combat ready divisions to the Army of the United States, and five tactical fighter wings to the Air Force of the United States; increased our strategic airlift capability by 75 percent; and increased our special counter–insurgency forces which are engaged now in South Viet–Nam by 600 percent.[9]

Although the Kennedy administration disapproved of some of the CIA's actions against Cuba, it maintained and expanded the Cuban policy begun in 1960 under Eisenhower by supporting the Bay of Pigs invasion early in 1961, setting up Operation Mongoose later that year, and instituting the economic embargo of Cuba in 1962.[10] Kennedy consistently promoted the interests of US investors over those of the native population in Latin America by opposing land reform and supporting military coups in Guatemala, Ecuador, the Dominican Republic and Brazil.[11]

9. A transcript of President Kennedy's speech to the Forth Worth Chamber of Commerce at the Texas Hotel on the morning of 22 November 1963 can be found at http://www.presidency.ucsb.edu/ws/index.php?pid=9538. For the escalation of the arms race under Kennedy, see Desmond Ball, *Politics and Force Levels: The Strategic Missile Program of the Kennedy Administration*, University of California Press, 1980.
10. For the Kennedy administration's activities against Cuba, see Warren Hinckle and William Turner, *The Fish is Red: The Story of the Secret War Against Castro*, Harper and Row, 1981, chapter 4; and Morris H. Morley, *Imperial State and Revolution: The United States and Cuba, 1952–1986*, Cambridge University Press, 1987, pp.148–154. For the prominent role of the Attorney General, Robert Kennedy, in setting up Operation Mongoose in contravention of both US and international law, see Raymond L. Garthoff, *Reflections on the Cuban Missile Crisis*, Brookings Institution, 1989, p.32.
11. See, in general, William Blum, *Killing Hope: US Military and CIA Interventions Since World War II*, Common Courage Press, 1995; and Thomas G. Paterson, ed., *Kennedy's Quest for Victory: American Foreign Policy, 1961–1963*, Oxford University Press, 1989. For a sympathetic view of Kennedy's policies in Latin America, see Stephen G. Rabe, *The Most Dangerous Area in the World: John F. Kennedy Confronts Communist Revolution in Latin America*, University of North Carolina Press, 1999. For the overthrow of the elected government of João Goulart in Brazil, which was planned and approved under Kennedy and carried out under Johnson, see Jan Knippers Black, *United States Penetration of Brazil*, University of Pennsylvania Press, 1977; and A.J. Langguth, *Hidden Terrors: The Truth about US Police Operations in Latin America*, Pantheon Books, 1978, pp.38–116. For the Kennedy administration's role in prioritising the control of internal dissent in Latin America, see an account by

The current state of the evidence shows that President Kennedy's policy toward Latin America, Vietnam and the Soviet Union did not go against the interests of US elites. Nor had he caused problems by implementing radical domestic policies. The Kennedy administration's civil rights legislation was a half–hearted response to a growing popular movement. Partly in order to ensure the support of segregationist senators, the administration consistently appointed segregationist judges, who actively opposed existing civil rights legislation, to federal courts in the southern states. One such judge said before his appointment that "I don't want these pinks, radicals and black voters to outvote those who are trying to preserve our segregationist laws and other traditions." Robert Kennedy, the Attorney General, stated that "I'm very proud of the judges that have been appointed. We looked into all of them for questions of integrity and whether they would uphold the law of the land."[12] Only after the violence in Birmingham, Alabama, early in 1963, did Kennedy treat the matter seriously, but even then he took the slower route of proposing new legislation rather than using his executive powers. There was little significant pressure on Kennedy to correct the most fundamental domestic inequalities of power, by altering the wealth distribution mechanisms to favour the general population rather than investors and owners. Kennedy showed no signs of independent action toward this; unsurprisingly so, since he personally benefitted from the existing mechanisms.

In third–world dictatorships, a *coup d'état* by one political force against another can succeed because power is highly concentrated and easily targetted. In relatively democratic, industrialised nation states, elite power is distributed sufficiently widely to make a violent *coup* difficult to achieve. Several institutional mechanisms allow domestic elites to keep short–term managers such as presidents in check. Owners of the mass media may put an unfavourable slant on news stories. Owners of capital may threaten to invest abroad rather than within the domestic economy, or to withdraw investment from particular projects. Political sponsors may threaten to withdraw financial and other forms of support. None of these measures was used to a significant extent against

one of the policy's planners: Charles Maechling, Jr., 'The Murderous Mind of the Latin American Military,' *Los Angeles Times*, 18 March 1982, part 2, p.11.

12. Howard Zinn, *SNCC: The New Abolitionists*, Beacon Press, 1964, pp.203–206.

Kennedy. If the dominant social institutions disapproved of the president's policies toward Vietnam, Cuba, domestic civil rights, or anything else, they evidently did not disapprove enough even to impose peaceful constraints on his actions.

An example of the peaceful replacement of a manager who had outlived his usefulness was President Johnson's *de facto* resignation following the decision of domestic economic elites early in 1968 to withdraw US forces from Vietnam. In response to the Tet Offensive, the US military calculated that 200,000 extra troops were required in Vietnam. The need to contain the widespread dissent at home meant that this many troops could not safely be spared. When the economic recession was taken into account, the war's benefits were now outweighed by its financial costs and the risk it posed to the existing concentration of domestic power. Johnson, the political face of the war, was given the news by his Senior Advisory Group on Vietnam on 26–27 March. He took the hint and announced four days later that he had decided not to seek re–election in 1968.[13]

President Kennedy must have been removed from office by an *ad hoc* group working outside the normal structures of institutional power. The JFK assassination was the result of a relatively small–scale conspiracy rather than a large–scale *coup d'état*. It is certainly conceivable that the conspirators included individual members of powerful domestic groups. Although President Kennedy had done little to annoy US economic and military elites in general, it is clear that there were many individuals associated with those elite groups who actively resented what they considered to be Kennedy's restraint over Cuba and, by extension, the Soviet Union. Such individuals would have been aware that their ambitions might be frustrated by Kennedy's probable re–election in 1964 to a further four years in office. They possessed not only a plausible motive but also the opportunity and the means to bring about his assassination, including the framing of a patsy. The strong evidence that President Kennedy's autopsy took place under military control suggests that some senior military figures were, at the very least, aware of the conspiracy behind his murder.

13. See e.g. David Halberstam, *The Best and the Brightest*, Random House, 1972, p.653. For the military's assessment of the problem of domestic dissent, see Noam Chomsky and Howard Zinn, ed., *The Pentagon Papers*, Senator Gravel Edition, Beacon Press, 1972, vol.4, esp. pp.541, 564.

The extent of their active involvement, however, remains unclear.[14]

It was obvious from very early on that President Kennedy's assassination was the result of a conspiracy. The transparent absurdity of the single–bullet theory by itself rules out a lone assassin as the culprit. Many conspiracy theorists, however, slip too easily into blaming institutions for the murder. Just because this or that employee of the CIA or the army or the Dallas police department may have played a part in the assassination, it does not follow that the CIA or the army or the police were the driving force behind the assassination.

The notion that Kennedy was a gallant hero, killed by domestic institutions in a *coup d'état*,[15] is almost as implausible as the notion that he was killed by a lone nut, Lee Harvey Oswald, firing an antiquated rifle with a broken telescopic sight. In both cases, the 'how' and the 'why' are missing. Oswald's motive for killing Kennedy, that "he was a general misanthropic fellow" who wanted to get his name in the history books,[16] is no more convincing than the proposition that the owners of the country would eliminate someone who was serving their interests faithfully, or that, if it suited their needs to replace Kennedy, they would risk doing so with violence rather than with any of the peaceful means at their disposal.

14. The evidence of Dr Pierre Finck, one of the pathologists at JFK's autopsy, makes it clear that senior military figures prevented the dissection of the president's back and throat wounds, and implies that they did this to avoid discovering definitive evidence of shots from more than one direction; see p.108 below.

15. For a rose–tinted interpretation of Kennedy as a saviour figure, motivated by high moral principles and cruelly cut down by the forces of evil, see James Douglass, *JFK and the Unspeakable: Why He Died and Why It Matters*, Orbis Books, 2008.

16. Lyndon Johnson asked Richard Russell, one of the Warren Commissioners, about Oswald's motive, and was told that "he was a general misanthropic fellow, ... he had never been satisfied anywhere he was on earth ... he had a desire to get his name in history and all." See Chapter 6, Lee Harvey Oswald's Motive, p.51 above.

Appendices

A The Medical Evidence

The medical evidence is the single most complex aspect of the JFK assassination, and is the source of many of the contradictions and ambiguities that have allowed the case to drag on for so long. Most of these contradictions and ambiguities are due to the nature of the autopsy, which appears at first sight to have been carried out to a scandalous level of incompetence. The most fundamental aspects of the medical evidence are the nature, size and location of President Kennedy's wounds, none of which were documented to a reasonable degree of precision.[1]

The autopsy took place during the evening of 22 November 1963 at Bethesda Naval Hospital Center, a military teaching institution near Washington, DC. Although many well–qualified forensic pathologists were available within a short distance of Bethesda, the

1. For the problems with the autopsy, see *HSCA Appendix*, vol.7, p.177; and Cyril H. Wecht, 'A Critique of President Kennedy's Autopsy,' in Josiah Thompson, *Six Seconds in Dallas: A Micro–Study of the Kennedy Assassination*, Bernard Geis Associates, 1967, pp.278–284. The most comprehensive and readable overviews of the medical evidence can be found in two articles in James Fetzer, ed., *Murder in Dealey Plaza: What We Know Now That We Didn't Know Then About The Death of JFK*, Catfeet Press, 2000: Gary L. Aguilar, 'The Converging Medical Case for Conspiracy in the Death of JFK' (pp.175–217); and David W. Mantik, 'Paradoxes of the JFK Assassination: The Medical Evidence Decoded' (pp.219–297). Harold Weisberg, *Never Again*, Carroll and Graf, 1995, and Charles Wilber, *Medicolegal Investigation of the President John F. Kennedy Murder*, Charles C. Thomas, 1978, provide the most reliable book–length treatments, but were published before the ARRB released many relevant documents. For a detailed account of the conduct of President Kennedy's autopsy and its interpretation by the Warren Commission, see Gerald McKnight, *Breach of Trust: How the Warren Commission Failed the Nation and Why*, University Press of Kansas, 2005, pp.153–180. The most complete online resource is Gary Aguilar and Kathy Cunningham, 'How Five Investigations into JFK's Medical/Autopsy Evidence Got it Wrong,' at http://www.history-matters.com/essays/jfkmed/How5Investigations/How5InvestigationsGotItWrong.htm.

pathologists chosen to conduct the autopsy were middle–ranking military officers whose only practical experience of forensic autopsies was a one–week course taken by one of the pathologists ten years earlier.[2]

Not all of the problems with the medical evidence are due to the inexperience of the pathologists. The written records from the autopsy are incomplete, and perhaps corrupt. The original autopsy report no longer exists; it was deliberately destroyed by Dr James Humes, the senior pathologist, after the murder of Lee Oswald. The reason given for the destruction, that the documents were spattered with the president's blood, is clearly untrue: some of the surviving documents are blood–stained, and the original report was written the day after the autopsy and would not have been contaminated.[3] The rewritten autopsy report includes measurements and other data that do not exist in the pathologists' surviving notes and diagrams.[4]

The photographs, or at least those that are publicly available, fail to provide clear and unambiguous views of any of Kennedy's wounds. In particular, they do not allow a definitive description of the wound or wounds to the head. The photographs do not match the recollections of the photographers and the pathologists. Both groups of participants remembered ordering or taking photographs that appear no longer to exist. The two photographers had been required to sign a receipt on the day of the autopsy and an inventory in 1966 stating that the photographic record was complete, but later testified that the documents were incorrect and that photographs were missing.[5] Among the missing photographs are at least two of the interior of Kennedy's torso[6] and one of his skull.[7] The brain, which might be expected to reveal information

2. The pathologists' qualifications: *HSCA Appendix*, vol.7, p.182.
3. Humes's destruction of the original autopsy report: testimony to ARRB, 13 February 1996, pp.136–138.
4. Rewritten autopsy report: *WR*, pp.538–546. The surviving notes from the autopsy: CE 397 (*WCHE*, vol.17, pp.29–48).
5. John Stringer: testimony to ARRB, 16 July 1996, pp.214–216; ARRB Medical Document 19, p.11. Floyd Riebe: testimony to ARRB, 7 May 1997, pp.53–54. The receipt: ARRB Medical Document 78. The inventory: ARRB Medical Document 13.
6. Stringer: testimony to ARRB, 16 July 1996, p.213; Dr Humes: ARRB Medical Document 19, p.7; *WCHE*, vol.2, p.363; Dr J. Thornton Boswell: ARRB Medical Document 26, p.6.
7. Dr Pierre Finck: ARRB Medical Document 30, pp.89–90.

about the number and direction of the fatal shot or shots, had gone missing by the time the House Select Committee on Assassinations inspected the medical evidence.[8]

The photographic record is not the only element of the autopsy that has attracted suspicions of foul play. One of the pathologists, Dr Pierre Finck, admitted under oath that he and his colleagues were ordered not to perform a dissection of the back and throat wounds, an elementary procedure that would almost certainly have determined whether the president's non–fatal injuries had been caused by one or more bullets, and from which direction or directions the bullet or bullets had come.

The autopsy took place several hours after President Kennedy's assassination and Lee Oswald's arrest. It was widely known at the time of the autopsy that Oswald had been inside the Texas School Book Depository, almost directly behind the president, during the shooting. The broadcast media had already reported the claims of eye–witnesses that shots had come from more than one direction, as well as a press conference at Parkland Hospital, during which one of the doctors who had treated the president claimed that the throat wound had been caused by a shot from the front:

Questioner : What was the entrance wound?

Dr Perry : There was an entrance wound in the neck. As regards the one in the head, I cannot say.

Questioner : Which way was the bullet coming on the neck wound? At him?

Dr Perry : It appeared to be coming at him.

Questioner : Doctor, describe the entrance wound. You think from the front in the throat?

Dr Perry : The wound appeared to be an entrance wound in the front of the throat; yes, that is correct.[9]

Those in charge of the autopsy would surely have been aware that President Kennedy's wounds may have been caused by more than one gunman, and that dissecting the wounds was likely to

8. *HSCA Appendix*, vol.7, p.177.
9. ARRB Medical Document 41, pp.5–6.

resolve the question one way or the other. Their refusal to allow the dissection can only reasonably be interpreted as a fear of discovering definitive evidence of conspiracy.

The two factors which forced the adoption of the lone–assassin explanation had not yet emerged. Evidence of Lee Oswald's impersonation in Mexico City, which implies that Oswald either had associates or was impersonated without his knowledge, did not reach Washington until several hours after the conclusion of the autopsy. Public suspicion of conspiracy, and the attendant public dissatisfaction with governmental institutions, was not yet widespread. Pierre Finck's testimony indicates that the high–ranking military officers who appeared to control the autopsy were already aware of the need to promote the lone–assassin explanation:

> **Mr Oser** : How many other military personnel were present at the autopsy in the autopsy room?
>
> **Col. Finck** : The autopsy room was quite crowded. It is a small autopsy room, and when you are called in circumstances like that to look at the wound of the President of the United States who is dead, you don't look around too much to ask people for their names and take notes on who they are and how many there are. I did not do so. The room was crowded with military and civilian personnel and federal agents, Secret Service agents, FBI agents, for part of the autopsy, but I cannot give you a precise breakdown as regards the attendance of the people in that autopsy room at Bethesda Naval Hospital.
>
> **Mr Oser** : Colonel, did you feel that you had to take orders from the Army General that was there directing the autopsy?
>
> **Col. Finck** : No, because there were others, there were Admirals.
>
> **Mr Oser** : There were Admirals?
>
> **Col. Finck** : Oh, yes, there were Admirals, and when you are a Lieutenant Colonel in the Army you just follow orders, and at the end of the autopsy we

were specifically told — as I recall it, it was by Admiral Kenney, the Surgeon General of the Navy — this is subject to verification — we were told not to discuss the case.

Mr Oser : You were told not to discuss the case?

Col. Finck : — to discuss the case without coordination with the Attorney General.[10]

...

Mr Oser : Doctor, speaking of the wound to the throat area of the President as you described it, after this bullet passed through the President's throat in the manner in which you described it, would the President have been able to talk?

Col. Finck : I don't know.

Mr Oser : Do you have an opinion?

Col. Finck : There are many factors influencing the ability to talk or not to talk after a shot.

Mr Oser : Did you have an occasion to dissect the track of that particular bullet in the victim as it lay on the autopsy table?

Col. Finck : I did not dissect the track in the neck.

Mr Oser : Why?

Col. Finck : This leads us into the disclosure of medical records.

Mr Oser : Your Honor, I would like an answer from the Colonel and I would ask The Court so to direct.

Judge : That is correct, you should answer, Doctor.

Col. Finck : We didn't remove the organs of the neck.

Mr Oser : Why not, Doctor?

Col. Finck : For the reason that we were told to examine the head wounds and that the —

10. *State of Louisiana vs. Clay L. Shaw*, Criminal District Court, Parish of Orleans, State of Louisiana, 198–059 1426(30) section C, transcript, pp.51–52.

Mr Oser : Are you saying someone told you not to dissect the track?

Judge : Let him finish his answer.

Col. Finck : I was told that the family wanted an examination of the head, as I recall, the head and the chest, but the prosectors in this autopsy didn't remove the organs of the neck, to my recollection.

Mr Oser : You have said that they did not. I want to know why didn't you as an autopsy pathologist attempt to ascertain the track through the body which you had on the autopsy table in trying to ascertain the cause or causes of death? Why?

Col. Finck : I had the cause of death.

Mr Oser : Why did you not trace the track of the wound?

Col. Finck : As I recall I didn't remove these organs from the neck.

Mr Oser : I didn't hear you.

Col. Finck : I examined the wounds but I didn't remove the organs of the neck.

Mr Oser : You said you didn't do this; I am asking you why didn't [you] do this as a pathologist?

Col. Finck : From what I recall I looked at the trachea, there was a tracheotomy wound the best I can remember, but I didn't dissect or remove these organs.

Mr Oser : Your Honor, I would ask Your Honor to direct the witness to answer my question. I will ask you the question one more time: Why did you not dissect the track of the bullet wound that you have described today and you saw at the time of the autopsy at the time you examined the body? Why? I ask you to answer that question.

Col. Finck : As I recall I was told not to, but I don't remember by whom.

Mr Oser : You were told not to but you don't remember by whom?

Col. Finck : Right.

Mr Oser : Could it have been one of the Admirals or one of the Generals in the room?

Col. Finck : I don't recall.

Mr Oser : Do you have any particular reason why you cannot recall at this time?

Col. Finck : Because we were told to examine the head and the chest cavity, and that doesn't include the removal of the organs of the neck.

Mr Oser : You are one of the three autopsy specialists and pathologists at the time, and you saw what you described as an entrance wound in the neck area of the President of the United States who had just been assassinated, and you were only interested in the other wound but not interested in the track through his neck, is that what you are telling me?

Col. Finck : I was interested in the track and I had observed the conditions of bruising between the point of entry in the back of the neck and the point of exit at the front of the neck, which is entirely compatible with the bullet path.

Mr Oser : But you were told not to go into the area of the neck, is that your testimony?

Col. Finck : From what I recall, yes, but I don't remember by whom.[11]

Another of the pathologists, J. Thornton Boswell, revealed three decades later that the Justice Department was greatly concerned by Finck's testimony. Carl Eardley, a Deputy Assistant Attorney General, got in touch with Boswell:

> He was really upset. He says, "J, we got to get somebody in New Orleans quick. Pierre is testifying, and he's really lousing everything up." . . . They showed me

11. *Ibid.*, pp.114–118.

> the transcript of Pierre's testimony for the past couple of days, and I spent all night reviewing that testimony. And it was this bit about the general. Jim [Humes, the chief pathologist] said, "Who's in charge here?" And when they asked Pierre in court who supervised and ran the autopsy, he says, "Some Army general."[12]

The two official interpretations of the medical evidence differ in crucial ways.[13] Because of the inadequate conduct of the autopsy and the poor preservation of the medical evidence, a plausible case can be made that President Kennedy's head wounds resulted from: one shot from behind, hitting him low down, near the external occipital protuberance, as the autopsy pathologists concluded; one shot from behind, hitting him four inches or ten centimetres higher, as the Clark Panel and the HSCA concluded; one shot from in front, hitting him above his right ear, as the Zapruder film and some of the X–rays indicate; and even two or more shots, from behind and from in front. Medical evidence can be cited to support all four contradictory statements.

One of the medical paradoxes is the apparent contrast between the accounts of the doctors in Dallas and those at the autopsy, concerning the damage to the head. The House Select Committee on Assassinations stated that, of the 26 witnesses at the autopsy who had given evidence, none agreed with the Dallas consensus of a large wound situated toward the back of President Kennedy's head, which implied a shot from the front, and that "it seems more probable that the observations of the Parkland doctors are incorrect."[14] This discrepancy gave rise to one of the very few pro–conspiracy books to have benefitted from generous and largely uncritical coverage in the media: David Lifton's *Best Evidence*.[15] Lifton interviewed many of the participants at the autopsy, and his book contains some useful information. His over–imaginative solution

12. J. Thornton Boswell: testimony to ARRB, 26 February 1996, pp.208–210.
13. *WR*, pp.86–91, and *HSCA Appendix*, vol.7, pp.80–134.
14. *HSCA Appendix*, vol.7, p.37.
15. David Lifton, *Best Evidence: Disguise and Deception in the Assassination of John F. Kennedy*, Macmillan, 1980. Page references that follow are from the Signet edition of 1992. For Lifton's other main contribution to the case, see James DiEugenio, *Destiny Betrayed: JFK, Cuba and the Garrison Case*, 2nd edition, Skyhorse Publishing, 2012, pp.188–189.

to the mystery is that at some point between its departure from Parkland Hospital in Dallas and its arrival at Bethesda Naval Hospital Center, Maryland, for the autopsy, the president's body had been surgically altered to hide evidence of shots from the front.

Lifton was inspired by a passage in the Sibert and O'Neill Report, the account by the two FBI agents who attended the autopsy. The agents reported that:

> The President's body was removed from the casket in which it had been transported and was placed on the autopsy table, at which time the complete body was wrapped in a sheet and the head area contained an additional wrapping which was saturated with blood. Following the removal of the wrapping, it was ascertained that the President's clothing had been removed and it was also apparent that a tracheotomy had been performed, as well as surgery of the head area, namely, in the top of the skull.[16]

Lifton described his reaction:

> I knew exactly what that meant — *this* was the missing piece of the puzzle.
>
> The Dallas doctors had operated only on the throat. No one had touched the President's head — certainly not with a surgical instrument.
>
> Yet those words, if true, meant that some time after the President was pronounced dead in Dallas, but before the coffin arrived in the Bethesda autopsy room, somebody had performed "surgery" on President Kennedy's corpse.
>
> I was exhilarated, terrified. I wanted to vomit.[17]

In an affidavit submitted to the House Select Committee on Assassinations in 1978, however, James Sibert explained that as the autopsy progressed, the pathologists revised their initial suspicions of "surgery of the head area":

16. ARRB Medical Document 44, p.3.
17. Lifton, *op. cit.*, p.201; emphasis in the original.

> When the body was first observed on the autopsy table, it was thought by the doctors that surgery had possibly been performed in the head area and such was reflected in my notes made at the time. However, this was determined not to be correct following detailed inspection and when the piece of bone found in the limousine was brought to the autopsy room during the latter stages of the autopsy.[18]

An unpublished but widely circulated manuscript by the late Roger Feinman, *Between the Signal and the Noise*, made a strong case against Lifton's notion of forgery to the president's corpse. The document includes useful background information about the world of the early JFK assassination researchers, as well as a rather petty, he–said–she–said account of a squabble between Feinman and Lifton. Feinman raised objections to four main aspects of Lifton's theory. Firstly, the apparent discrepancies between the medical witnesses at Parkland and at Bethesda can be explained without having to assume foul play. Secondly, Lifton proposed that all the shots were fired from the front: "to be able to shoot the President, retrieve the bullets, and insure that afterward it appeared the shots came from behind, the real bullets had to be fired from the front."[19] The only wound that was caused by a bullet whose trajectory is beyond dispute was the wound to Governor Connally's torso: a bullet entered his back and came out of his chest. Lifton fails to deal with this fundamental contradiction, as others have pointed out: "Lifton makes no attempt to explain Connally's wounds within the terms of his theory. He does not seem to notice the problem at all."[20] Thirdly, the body was supposedly altered in order to fool the pathologists into believing that all the shots came from behind, but the pathologists may already have been aware that Kennedy's throat wound was the result of a shot from in front. Feinman argues that Dr George Burkley, the only medically qualified person to have been present both at Parkland Hospital and the autopsy, had been in the emergency room while a

18. James Sibert, Affidavit to HSCA, 24 October 1978, p.4.
19. Lifton, *op. cit.*, p.400.
20. Thomas Powers and Alan Rich, 'Robbing the Grave,' *New York Magazine*, 23 February 1981, p.46, cited in Roger Feinman, *Between the Signal and the Noise*, chapter 5. The wound to Connally's torso: CE 392 (*WCHE*, vol.17, p.16).

tracheotomy had been performed over the wound.[21] Fourthly, the wound in Kennedy's back was supposedly constructed to implicate Oswald, but its location exonerates him: it is too low to make the single–bullet theory credible.

Feinman took Lifton's notion that the alteration of the body was an integral part of the plot, and pointed out the enormous extra complexity and potential for disaster that the notion entails. Rather than hiring snipers to shoot President Kennedy only from in front, and hiring surgeons to construct wounds in his back and head to mimic shots from behind, and hiring teams to kidnap the corpse and transport it to and from some unnamed location, all of which Lifton proposed, why not simply hire a sniper to shoot him from behind in the first place?

Lifton was not the first or the last writer to suggest that Kennedy's body had been tampered with.[22] Feinman pointed out that this type of thinking causes more harm than good. The invention of implausible and unnecessary conspiracies to resolve conflicts in the evidence does not bring an explanation for the assassination any closer. Propagandists for the lone–nut hypothesis can point to the relative credibility of their beliefs when compared to the notion that an unspecified number of unidentified conspirators using an unexplained method whisked the president's body away from under the noses of all the people on Air Force One as well as the ground crew and the journalists and sightseers who were watching the plane: "If my analysis was correct, the President's body was inside the Dallas casket when it was put aboard Air Force One at 2:18, but was no longer inside the casket at 2:47, as the plane rolled down the runway."[23] The real problem with *Best Evidence* is not the believability or otherwise of its thesis but rather the media's decision to promote this particular book as a representative of the many critical works written about the assassination.[24]

21. Feinman, *op. cit.*, chapter 8.
22. The earliest published account seems to be Fred T. Newcomb and Perry Adams, 'Did Someone Alter the Medical Evidence?', *Skeptic*, Special Issue no.9 (September–October 1975), pp.24–27.
23. Lifton, *op. cit.*, p.790. Against Lifton, see Joel Grant, 'Body Snatchers at Love Field?' at http://mcadams.posc.mu.edu/b_snatch.htm.
24. For more criticism of the body–alteration theory, see David Wrone, *The Zapruder Film: Reframing JFK's Assassination*, University Press of Kansas, 2003, pp.134–137; and Harold Weisberg's unpublished manuscript, *Autopsy of a JFK Assassination Best*

The autopsy witnesses' testimony had been classified by the HSCA in 1978. When the evidence was finally released to the public, 30 years after the assassination, it turned out that rather than 26 autopsy witnesses testifying against the wound at the rear of the head, the HSCA had taken evidence from only 12. Those 12 witnesses at the autopsy had actually agreed with the earliest, incorrupt evidence of the witnesses in Dallas: the wound extended into the back of the head. The HSCA had simply lied, and the theory of bodily alteration was unnecessary.[25]

Seller: Best Evidence as Bad Evidence, available at the Harold Weisberg Archive at Hood College, Frederick, Maryland, and online at http://jfk.hood.edu/.
25. For the HSCA's treatment of the witnesses, see Gary L. Aguilar, *op. cit.*, pp.197–200.

B Neutron Activation Analysis

Neutron activation analysis is currently the most sensitive and reliable method of measuring quantities of elements within compounds. 74 elements are susceptible to NAA, which can detect quantities in the range of parts per billion. NAA usually takes place within nuclear reactors. The process is as follows. A sample is subjected to bombardment by neutrons, which causes individual nuclei within the sample to become radioactive. As each radioactive nucleus decays, it gives off gamma rays, whose distinct properties allow individual isotopes to be identified. The gamma rays are measured to determine the rate of decay for each isotope. The rate of decay, measured against that from a comparative sample of an element, allows the concentration of that element within the original sample to be determined.[1]

Neutron activation analysis has been used to examine two types of physical evidence in the JFK assassination: paraffin wax casts and bullet fragments. Paraffin wax casts were taken of the hands and right cheek of Lee Harvey Oswald, the only official suspect in the murder. The casts were tested by NAA within weeks of the assassination to see whether they contained incriminating quantities of gunpowder residues. Similar tests were done on a controlled sample of casts from marksmen who fired a gun of the same type as that found on the sixth floor of the Texas School Book Depository.

Fragments of bullets were recovered from President Kennedy's car, from Kennedy himself, and from Governor John Connally, who

1. For details, see e.g. Michael D. Glascock, 'Overview of Neutron Activation Analysis' at http://archaeometry.missouri.edu/naa_overview.html.

had been sitting directly in front of the president. An almost intact bullet, Commission Exhibit 399, nicknamed the magic bullet because of the large amount of damage it is supposed to have caused and the elaborate trajectory it is supposed to have taken, had apparently been found on a stretcher used by Connally. In 1977, the fragments and CE 399 were tested by NAA to see how many bullets the fragments had come from, and whether the fragments from Connally's wrist had come from the magic bullet.

The casts from Lee Harvey Oswald's hands and cheek were subjected first of all to the normal chemical test, using diphenylbenzidine. According to an FBI memo, "The results show Punctate traces of nitrate found in the paraffin on the right and left hands consistent with that of a person who handled or fired a firearm. The paraffin of right check [*sic*] showed no traces of nitrate."[2] The absence of traces of nitrate on his cheek suggested that he had not fired a rifle that day.

Senior officials at the Atomic Energy Commission got in touch with the FBI, and made several offers to perform NAA tests on the paraffin casts and the bullet fragments. Grudgingly, the FBI agreed, noting that Oswald's murder had ensured that the tests would never be examined at trial, and that "any such examinations will, of course, be with the strict understanding that the information and dissemination of the results will be under complete FBI control."[3] The tests were performed in December 1963 and January 1964. The FBI informed the Warren Commission of the tests in March, pointing out only that "as a result of these [neutron activation analysis] examinations, the deposits found on the paraffin casts from the hands and cheek of Oswald could not be specifically associated with the rifle cartridges."[4]

The Commission did not follow up the matter until early September, when the *Warren Report* was about to be published. The Commission called its final witness, John F. Gallagher, the FBI laboratory specialist who had overseen the NAA examinations of the paraffin casts and the bullet fragments.[5] As with the large majority of the Warren Commission's witnesses, the only people present

2. Result of chemical test: FBI HQ JFK Assassination File, 62–109060–8.
3. Under FBI control: FBI HQ JFK File, 62–109060–5.
4. Results of NAA of casts: FBI HQ Oswald File, 105–82555–94.
5. John Gallagher: *WCHE*, vol.15, pp.746–52.

were the witness, a stenographer, and the questioner, who in this case was Norman Redlich, one of the Commission's staff attorneys. Before the interview, Gallagher and Redlich discussed the areas that would be included and those that would be ignored.[6] Redlich limited his questioning to Oswald's paraffin casts, and carefully avoided asking for details and precise measurements. Neither man mentioned the fact that NAA tests had also been applied to the bullet fragments.

Gallagher did point out that the cast of Oswald's right cheek possessed traces of barium and antimony on the outside as well as on the inside. Evidently the cast had become contaminated. The existence of residues on the outside implied that at least some of the material on the inside was also the result of contamination. No figures were specified, but Gallagher implies that the quantities were minimal:

> **Mr Redlich** : Were you able to make determination as to whether the barium and antimony present on the inside cast was more than would be expected in the case of a person who had not fired a weapon or handled a fired weapon?
>
> **Mr Gallagher** : I found that there was more barium and antimony on the inside surface of the cast than you would find on the cheek of an individual who had recently washed his cheek.[7]

Neutron activation analysis supported the conclusion of the chemical test: there were no incriminating quantities of gunpowder residues on Lee Harvey Oswald's right cheek. Redlich and Gallagher had succeeded in obscuring the significance of the lack of residues on Oswald's cheek, and in keeping out of the official record the NAA tests on the bullet fragments. They had also neglected to mention that controlled tests had taken place on the paraffin casts. This became public knowledge when the *New York Times* quoted a scientist at a conference in Glasgow:

6. Rehearsal: *ibid.*, p.752.
7. Small quantities of barium and antimony: *ibid.*, p.751.

> Dr Vincent P. Guinn, head of the activation analysis program of the General Atomic division of Genreal Dynamics Corporation, has been working on the problem with the Federal Bureau of Investigation. "In the case of murder or any crime involving a gun," Dr Guinn said, "there is a paraffin test where a wax impression is taken of the hand and cheeks. There is a need for a better procedure and about three years ago we began working on activation analysis. We bought a similar rifle from the same shop as Oswald and conducted two parallel tests."[8]

Harold Weisberg, perhaps the most dogged of the first generation of researchers, sued under the Freedom of Information Act for the records of the various neutron activation analyses. The case dragged on for 17 years, with the Department of Justice claiming that public knowledge of the data was not in the interests of 'national security.' Eventually, nearly twenty years after the assassination, some of the results of the NAA tests were made available to Weisberg. He concluded that there had in fact been seven controlled tests: "The tests given me show that in seven 'control' cases where others had fired a rifle this evidence was left on the cheeks."[9] As might be expected, given the authorities' unwillingness to release the documents, the control tests appear to prove that neutron activation analysis can be expected to show substantial quantities of barium and antimony on the cheek of anyone who had fired a rifle of the same type as that found on the sixth floor of the TSBD. The absence of such quantities on Oswald's cheek implies that he almost certainly did not fire a rifle on the day of the assassination.[10]

Weisberg's legal action disclosed that the Atomic Energy Commission had tested not only Oswald's paraffin casts but also several

8. *New York Times*, 28 August 1964, p.32.
9. Harold Weisberg, *Post Mortem: JFK Assassination Cover–Up Smashed*, Weisberg, 1975, p.437.
10. The court case is *Weisberg v. Energy Research and Development Administration and the Department of Justice*, Civil Action 75–226; by the time of the court case, the Atomic Energy Commission had been absorbed into the Energy Research and Development Administration. The documents, which still await expert appraisal, are available in the Harold Weisberg Archive, Hood College, Frederick, Maryland; and online at http://jfk.hood.edu/.

Table B.1: **Parts per million of antimony in JFK bullet samples**

Specimen	Description	Antimony, ppm
CE 399	Magic bullet	833 ± 9
CE 842	Fragment from Connally's wrist	797 ± 7
CE 840	3 fragments from rear floor of car	642 ± 6
CE 843	Fragment from JFK's head	621 ± 4
CE 567	Fragment from front car seat	602 ± 4

bullet fragments. The House Select Committee on Assassinations in 1977 felt obliged to deal with the matter. Dr Vincent Guinn, who by this time was at the University of California at Irvine, was given the task of subjecting various bullet fragments to neutron activation analysis. Guinn ran NAA tests on five samples. Concentrations of antimony (Sb), in parts per million, are given in Table B.1.[11]

Guinn concluded that the six fragments came from just two bullets. CE 842, one of the fragments from Connally's wrist, can be matched to CE 399, the magic bullet, because both have relatively high concentrations of Sb. CE 840 and CE 567, the four fragments found in the car, can be matched to CE 843, one of the fragments from JFK's head, because all five have relatively low concentrations of Sb. As he explained to the HSCA:

> Two of the samples have indistinguishable compositions, indicating that they came from the same bullet, and the other three particles are evidently samples from another bullet.... There is no evidence for three bullets, four bullets, or anything more than two, but there is clear evidence that there are two.[12]

Guinn pointed out two characteristics of the Western Cartridge Company's Mannlicher Carcano bullets. They displayed variable

11. CE 399: *WCHE*, vol.17, p.49. CE 567: *ibid.*, p.256. CE 840: *ibid.*, p.840. CE 842 and CE 843: *ibid.*, p.841. CE 840 figures are combined, with standard deviations calculated by Spiegelman *et al.*; see n.15 below.
12. Two bullets: *HSCA Appendix*, vol.1, p.504.

concentrations of antimony within a batch, in contrast to his samples of other bullets, in which the concentration of antimony is consistent within a batch. The amount of antimony is consistent within each Mannlicher Carcano bullet.

> You simply do not find a wide variation in composition within individual WCC Mannlicher–Carcano bullets, but you do find wide compositional differences from bullet to bullet for this kind of bullet lead. Thus, when you find two specimens that agree this closely, you can say it looks indeed like they are pieces from the same bullet.[13]

The HSCA depended upon Guinn's expert testimony to support the single–bullet theory, which is fundamental to the case that all the injuries were caused by only one gunman:

> The single bullet theory was substantiated by the findings of a neutron activation analysis performed for the committee.... It was highly likely that the injuries to Governor Connally's wrist were caused by the bullet found on the stretcher in Parkland Hospital....
>
> The neutron activation analysis further supported the single bullet theory by indicating that there was evidence of only two bullets among the fragments recovered from the limousine and its occupants. The consultant who conducted the analysis concluded that it was "highly likely" that CE 399 and the fragments removed from Governor Connally's wrist were from one bullet; [and] that one of the two fragments recovered from the floor of the limousine and the fragment removed from the President's brain during the autopsy were from a second bullet. Neutron activation analysis showed no evidence of a third bullet among those fragments large enough to be tested.[14]

13. One bullet: *ibid.*, p.505.
14. *HSCA Report*, p.45.

Two articles by metallurgists and statisticians, however, indicated flaws with Vincent Guinn's methodology and his conclusions.[15] As the second article pointed out:

> Random matches to assassination fragments of bullets from the same box are not as rare as Dr Guinn testified. Most importantly, our studies and analyses of individual bullet compositions, bullet lead source compositions and compositional mixtures in packaged retail boxes show that Dr Guinn's statements about the uniqueness of individual bullets from the brand of bullets believed to be used in the assassination are seriously flawed.[16]

The authors purchased boxes from two separate lots of Mannlicher Carcano bullets:

> We then analyzed 10 bullets from each box. The measurement approach was similar to that used by Dr Guinn except that we used more appropriate standards, a known quality control procedure, and analyzed physical samples having a known geometry. *One of the bullets analyzed matched an assassination fragment.* We also found that many bullets in the same box have matching antimony and silver levels; this discovery is contrary to Dr Guinn's testimony that based on these two elements virtually every bullet of this type is unique.[17]

Bullets do not contain pure lead. Supplies of bullet lead come mostly from recycled car batteries, and contain trace quantities of elements such as copper, tin, arsenic and antimony in varying

15. Erik Randich and Patrick M. Grant, 'Proper Assessment of the JFK Assassination Bullet Lead Evidence from Metallurgical and Statistical Perspectives,' *Journal of Forensic Sciences*, vol.51 no.4 (July 2006), pp.717–728, available at http://e-reports-ext.llnl.gov/pdf/337848.pdf (PDF: 1 MB); and Cliff Spiegelman, William A. Tobin, William D. James, Simon J. Sheather, Stuart Wexler and D. Max Roundhill, 'Chemical and Forensic Analysis of JFK Assassination Bullet Lots: Is a Second Shooter Possible?', *The Annals of Applied Statistics*, vol.1 no.2 (2007), pp.287–301, available at http://arxiv.org/pdf/0712.2150 (PDF: 239 KB).
16. Spiegelman *et al.*, *op. cit.*, p. 289.
17. *Ibid.*, p. 290; emphasis in original.

amounts. The manufacturing process for bullets without copper or steel jackets includes a tightly controlled extra amount of antimony, usually comprising up to five percent of the alloy, which hardens the lead sufficiently to allow the bullets to function without a jacket.

Guinn's control group had comprised three bullets without jackets. Each bullet contained an almost identical proportion of antimony to lead. The Western Cartridge Company's Mannlicher Carcano bullets, on the other hand, were jacketed, and contained variable proportions of antimony and other trace elements. Guinn noted the variable proportions of antimony in the JFK bullet fragments, and mistakenly assumed that this variability was a feature of that brand of bullet. In fact, it is a feature of all types of jacketed bullets. He also claimed that the antimony within an individual bullet is distributed evenly. This turned out not to be true of the Western Cartridge Company bullets, in which antimony tends to be concentrated around crystals of lead.

The more recent research indicates that levels of antimony in bullet fragments have no necessary relation to the number of bullets from which those fragments originated. Fragments which contain similar levels of antimony could come from one bullet, but could instead come from several bullets. Fragments which contain differing levels of antimony could come from several bullets, but could instead come from different areas within one bullet. In short, neutron activation analysis cannot be used to determine the origin of bullet fragments. The technique is no longer used by the FBI for this purpose.[18]

Neutron activation analysis of the bullet fragments has two consequences for any study of the JFK assassination. There is no reason to suppose that the bullet fragments retrieved from Governor Connally's wrist have any connection with CE 399, the magic bullet. The absence of damage to the base of CE 399 makes it extremely unlikely that the fragments of lead came from that bullet, which in any case appears to have been entered into evidence fraudulently at a later date. If Governor Connally's wrist wound was not caused by the bullet which injured President Kennedy,

18. For the FBI's misuse of NAA, see Paul C. Giannelli, 'Comparative Bullet Lead Analysis: A Retrospective,' *Criminal Law Bulletin*, vol.47 no.2 (September 2011), pp.306–315.

the single–bullet theory is false, and more than one gunman must have been involved in the assassination. Nor is there any reason to suppose that the two large fragments of copper–jacketed bullets retrieved from the presidential limousine, CE 567 and CE 840, have any connection with the shot or shots to President Kennedy's head. The presence of dozens of tiny particles of bullet lead in JFK's skull suggests very strongly that a non–jacketed bullet had been used. Such a bullet could not have been associated with any of the shells found in the TSBD. Again, the implication is that more than one gunman was involved.[19]

In addition to the paraffin casts and the bullet fragments, a third type of physical evidence had been suggested as a subject for neutron activation analysis: the damaged areas at the front of President Kennedy's shirt and on his tie. The FBI declined to use NAA on the clothes. As J. Edgar Hoover explained in a letter to J. Lee Rankin:

> Would neutron activation analyses show if a bullet passed through the hole in the front of President Kennedy's shirt near the collar button area and also if a bullet passed through the material of his tie? Neutron activation is a sensitive analytical technique to determine elements present in a substance. During the course of the spectrographic examinations previously conducted of the fabric surrounding the hole in the front of the shirt, including the tie, no copper was found in excess of that present elsewhere in undamaged areas of the shirt and tie. Therefore, no copper was found which could be attributed to projectile fragments.
>
> It is not felt that the increased sensitivity of neutron activation analyses would contribute substantially

19. For more about NAA and the JFK assassination, see: Donald B. Thomas, *Hear No Evil: Social Constructivism and the Forensic Evidence in the Kennedy Assassination*, Mary Ferrell Foundation Press, 2010, pp.95–115; Gerald D. McKnight, *Breach of Trust: How the Warren Commission Failed the Nation and Why*, University Press of Kansas, 2005, pp.198–212; and Gary Aguilar, 'Is Vincent Bugliosi Right that Neutron Activation Analysis Proves Oswald's Guilt?' at http://www.maryferrell.org/wiki/index.php/Essay_-_Is_Vincent_Bugliosi_Right_that_Neutron_Activation_Analysis_Proves_Oswalds_Guilt.

> to the understanding of the origin of this hole and frayed area.[20]

In other words, normal spectroscopic examination had already shown that the cuts in JFK's shirt collar and tie had almost certainly not been caused by a copper–jacketed bullet, and Hoover feared that NAA would only confirm this conclusion.[21] For the Warren Commission's single–bullet theory to be credible, it was necessary for a bullet to have caused the two slits in the front of the shirt and the small nick in the tie. In its *Report*, the Commission mentioned that traces of copper were found by spectroscopic examination around the hole in the back of the shirt, but failed to mention the absence of copper around the slits in the front. It dishonestly left open the possibility that the damage to the front may have been caused by a bullet.[22]

20. NAA on shirt: CD 525, p.2.
21. For the results of the spectroscopic examination, see FBI HQ JFK Assassination File, 62–109060–14.
22. *WR*, p.92.

C Grassy Knoll Witnesses

About forty witnesses to the assassination of President Kennedy claimed either to have heard gunshots from the infamous grassy knoll in the northwest corner of Dealey Plaza, or to have seen smoke or smelled gunpowder in that area. Several of these witnesses were interviewed by newspaper, radio and television reporters immediately after the assassination. The interviews were influential in generating doubts about the lone–gunman theory. Many other interviews have been carried out in the years since the assassination, almost all of them by private researchers.

Examination of photographs and home movies suggests that there were perhaps as many as 600 people in Dealey Plaza at the time of the assassination. Official interviews or statements exist for around 200 of these witnesses. Because the Warren Commission performed no investigation of its own, almost all of the witnesses who testified before the Commission were chosen from those who had already made official statements. The other 400 or so, including many of the spectators nearest to the president, were never interviewed officially at all. Few of these missing witnesses were even identified. Representatives of the Warren Commission were told, for example, that many of the prisoners in the county jail, which overlooked Dealey Plaza, had witnessed the assassination. None of the prisoners appears to have been questioned.[1]

In many cases, the witnesses who were questioned were not asked about the origin of the shots. Of those who were asked, probably a small majority claimed that the shots came from the general direction of the Texas School Book Depository. A handful

1. *WCHE*, vol.15, pp.525–526.

of people claimed to have heard shots from more than one direction. Many had no opinion.

There are some curiosities within the evidence. Emmett Hudson, the only man identified out of the three standing on the steps leading up to the fence on the grassy knoll, claimed that all the shots came from the general direction of the Texas School Book Depository.[2] Buell Wesley Frazier, Billy Lovelady and Otis Williams, three men who were standing on the front steps of the TSBD, directly underneath the supposed sniper's nest, claimed that all the shots came from the general direction of the knoll.[3] Charles Brehm, who had an excellent view of the assassination, either changed his mind or was misquoted. He was reported in the *Dallas Times Herald* on the evening of 22 November as thinking that "the shots came from in front of or beside the President." The FBI two days later stated that "it seemed quite apparent to him that the shots came from one or two buildings back at the corner of Elm and Houston Streets."[4] Arnold Rowland thought the shots had come from the knoll, despite already having seen a man in the southwest window of the sixth floor of the TSBD, holding a gun.[5] Kenneth O'Donnell and David Powers nominated the TSBD in their testimony, but believed in private that shots had come from the knoll.[6]

Witnesses' perceptions of the direction and number of shots may be distorted by the nature of the gunshots and the social information received by the witnesses. A gunshot will produce three distinct sources of sound: the supersonic shock wave of the bullet, the blast from the muzzle, and reverberations from the surroundings. The detection of these sounds will vary according to three factors: the distance of the observer from the source of the shot; the angle of the bullet's path in relation to the position of the observer; and the nature of any physical objects that generate echoes. Experiments carried out on behalf of the House Select Committee on Assassinations demonstrated "how listeners can misjudge the source and number of shots in such a space" as Dealey Plaza.[7]

2. Emmett Hudson: *WCHE*, vol.7, p.560 and p.564. His earliest statements, however, are ambiguous: *WCHE*, vol.19, p.481; *cf.* CD 5, p.30 and *HSCA Report*, pp.605–606.
3. See below for: Frazier, p.136; Lovelady, p.140; and Williams, p.150.
4. Charles Brehm: CE 1425 (*WCHE*, vol.22, p.837).
5. Arnold Rowland: *WCHE*, vol.2, pp.171–173.
6. O'Donnell and Powers: see p.143 below.
7. *HSCA Appendix*, vol.8, p.131.

Social information is likely to have affected witness statements about the directions of shots in two ways. Many of those who ran toward the grassy knoll immediately after the shooting may have done so not because they had detected shots from that area but because the people around them were running in that direction. Many of those who claimed that shots came only from the TSBD did so some time after the event, when newspaper, television and radio reports had consistently named the TSBD as the only source of the shots.

Media reports are also likely to have influenced witnesses' accounts of the number of shots that were fired. As the *Warren Report* admitted, "Soon after the three empty cartridges were found, officials at the scene decided that three shots were fired, and that conclusion was widely circulated by the press. The eyewitness testimony may be subconsciously colored by the extensive publicity given the conclusion that three shots were fired."[8] There are other reasons to suppose that such testimony may be inaccurate. The HSCA researchers pointed out that:

> The buildings around the Plaza caused strong reverberations, or echoes, that followed the initial sound by from 0.5 to 1.5 sec. While these reflections caused no confusion to our listeners, who were prepared and expected to hear them, they may well have inflated the number of shots reported by the surprised witnesses during the assassination.[9]

In other words, the number of shots reported by witnesses is likely to be greater than the number of shots actually fired. A large majority of those witnesses who specified a number claimed that three shots had been fired. This cannot plausibly be an overestimate; it is not credible that the known injuries can have been caused by fewer than three bullets. If there had indeed been exactly three shots fired, it is likely that many witnesses would have been under the impression at the time that more than three had been fired. As with the witnesses' statements about the source of the shots, almost all of the statements about the number of shots

8. *WR*, pp.110–111.
9. *HSCA Appendix*, vol.8, pp.135–137.

Table C.1: **Witnesses to shots from TSBD and grassy knoll**

Author	**TSBD**	**Grassy Knoll**
Harold Feldman	32	51
Josiah Thompson	25	33
House Select Committee on Assassinations	48	20
Stewart Galanor	48	52
John McAdams	56	34

were made after the media had begun to report consistently that exactly three shots had been fired. It is not unreasonable to suppose that the number of shots reported by witnesses is likely to be influenced more by social information than by actual experience.[10]

Several researchers have tried to determine how many witnesses declared that shots came from the general direction of the knoll, or the TSBD, or both directions, or neither. Because of the frequent imprecision both of the witnesses' answers and the questions they were asked, it was easy for researchers to impose their own preferences on the figures. Consequently, the totals vary widely, as seen in Table C.1.[11]

Most of the evidence quoted below falls into four categories: contemporaneous reports by journalists who were in Dealey Plaza; statements to the police or sheriff's deputies within hours of the assassination; statements to the FBI, mostly within a few days of the assassination; and interviews by the Warren Commission's staff at-

10. For the number of shots reported by witnesses, see *ibid.*, p.142. Andrew M. Mason, 'Witness Evidence in the JFK Assassination,' at http://www.spmlaw.ca/jfk/shot_pattern_evidence.pdf (PDF: 90 KB), places great weight on the fact that many of the witnesses testified independently to hearing three shots in a specific pattern, but fails to take into account those witnesses' exposure to the media's promotion of the three–shot doctrine.

11. Harold Feldman, 'Fifty–One Witnesses,' *Minority of One*, March 1965. Josiah Thompson, *Six Seconds in Dallas: A Micro–Study of the Kennedy Assassination*, Bernard Geis Associates, 1967, pp.254–270. *HSCA Appendix*, vol.2, p.122. Stewart Galanor, *Cover–Up*, Kestrel Books, 1998, pp.72, 171–180. Galanor has compiled the most complete online record of witnesses in Dealey Plaza: http://www.history-matters.com/analysis/witness/index.htm. John McAdams at http://mcadams.posc.mu.edu/shots.htm.

torneys several months after the assassination. Some of the official evidence first became publicly available when the Warren Commission's *Hearings and Exhibits* were issued in November 1964. Some of it was not published at all, but was placed in the National Archives, and was only discovered at a later date. Access to the evidence was not helped by the fact that the witnesses' statements and testimony were scattered throughout many of the 26 volumes of the *Hearings and Exhibits*.

Here is a list, in alphabetical order by surname, and no doubt incomplete, of those witnesses to President Kennedy's assassination who claimed or implied that one or more shots came from the general direction of the grassy knoll. Two more categories of witnesses follow this list. Several other witnesses gave less definitive statements that may nevertheless be interpreted as evidence of shots from the grassy knoll. Four witnesses of varying degrees of credibility, Gordon Arnold, Cheryl McKinnon, Lee Bowers, and Ed Hoffman, also claimed to have experienced shots or other sinister activity on the grassy knoll.

Victoria Adams

Victoria Adams was watching the motorcade from a window on the fourth floor of the Texas School Book Depository.

> She believed the sound came from toward the right of the building, rather than from the left and above as it must have been according to subsequent information disseminated by the news services.[12]

> It seemed as if it came from the right below rather than from the left above.[13]

Danny Garcia Arce

Danny Arce, a colleague of Lee Oswald, was on the north side of Elm Street, near the TSBD.

12. Victoria Adams: CD 5, p.39 (24 November 1963). For more about Victoria Adams, see Barry Ernest, *The Girl on the Stairs: My Search for a Missing Witness to the Assassination of John F. Kennedy*, Createspace, 2011.
13. *WCHE*, vol.6, p.388 (7 April 1964).

> To the best of my knowledge there were three shots and they came from the direction of the railroad tracks near the parking lot at the west end of the Depository Building.[14]

Mr Ball : Where did you make out the direction of the sound?

Mr Arce : Yeah, I thought they came from the railroad tracks to the west of the Texas School Book Depository.

...

Mr Ball : Now, it sounded to you that the shots came from what direction?

Mr Arce : From the tracks on the west deal.

...

Mr Ball : Did you look back at the building?

Mr Arce : No, I didn't think they came from there. I just looked directly to the railroad tracks and all the people started running up there and I just ran along with them.[15]

Virginia Baker (née Rackley)

Virginia Rackley, who got married shortly after the assassination, was standing on the north side of Elm Street close to the main entrance to the TSBD.

> It sounded as though these sounds were coming from the direction of the Triple Underpass, and looking in that direction after the first shot she saw something bounce from the roadway in front of the Presidential automobile and now presumes it was a bullet bouncing off the pavement....

14. Danny Garcia Arce: CE 1381, p.5 (*WCHE*, vol.22, p.634) (18 March 1964).
15. *WCHE*, vol.6, pp.365–366 (7 April 1964).

Rackley stated that she did not look up at the Texas School Book Depository building since she did not think that the sounds were coming from that building.[16]

Mr Liebeler : Did you have any idea where they [the shots] were coming from?

Mrs Baker : Well, the way it sounded — it sounded like it was coming from — there was a railroad track that runs behind the building — there directly behind the building and around, so I guess it would be by the underpass, the triple underpass, and there is a railroad track that runs back out there.

...

Mr Liebeler : And you say there are some railroad tracks back in there; is that right?

Mrs Baker : Yes.

Mr Liebeler : Immediately behind Dealey Plaza away from Elm Street?

Mrs Baker : Yes.

Mr Liebeler : And is that where you thought the shots came from?

Mrs Baker : Yes.[17]

Jane Berry

Jane Berry was standing on the north side of Elm Street a few yards west of the TSBD.

> Everyone was very excited and no one seemed to know where the shot had come from. It sounded as if it had been fired from a position west of where she was standing.[18]

16. Virginia Rackley: CD 5, pp.66–67 (24 November 1963). Linguistic note: although almost every British reader will know that a 'pavement' in the UK is a 'sidewalk' in the US, not all will be aware that in US English, the word 'pavement' refers to the hard surface of a road.
17. *WCHE*, vol.7, p.510 (22 March 1964).
18. Jane Berry: CD 5, p.42 (24 November 1964).

Charles Brehm

Charles Brehm was standing with his wife and young son on the south side of Elm Street, just a few yards from President Kennedy at the moment of the fatal shot.

> The witness Brehm was shaking uncontrollably as he further described the shooting. "The first shot must not have been too solid, because he just slumped. Then on the second shot he seemed to fall back."
>
> Brehm seemed to think the shots came from in front of or beside the President. He explained the President did not slump forward as he would have after being shot from the rear. The book depository building stands in the rear of the President's location at the time of the shooting.[19]

Ochus Campbell

Ochus Campbell, the vice–president of the Texas School Book Depository Company, was standing with Roy Truly on the north side of Elm Street, about 30 feet from the front entrance to the TSBD.

> Campbell says he ran toward a grassy knoll to the west of the building, where he thought the sniper had hidden.[20]

> Mr. CAMPBELL advised he had viewed the Presidential Motorcade and subsequently heard the shots being fired from a point which he thought was near the railroad tracks located over the viaduct on Elm Street.[21]

> I heard shots being fired from a point which I thought was near the railroad tracks located over the viaduct on Elm street. I . . . had no occasion to look back at the Texas School Book Depository building as I thought the shots had come from the west.[22]

19. Charles Brehm: *Dallas Times Herald*, 22 November 1963, p.1.
20. Ochus Campbell: *Dallas Morning News*, 23 November 1963.
21. CD 5, p.336 (26 November 1963).
22. CE 1381, p.14 (*WCHE*, vol.22, p.638) (19 March 1964).

Faye Chism

Faye and John Chism were standing close to the Stemmons Freeway sign on the north side of Elm Street.

> It came from what I thought was behind us.[23]

John Chism

> I looked behind me, to see whether it was a fireworks display or something. And then I saw a lot of people running for cover, behind the embankment there back up on the grass.[24]

> On hearing the second shot he definitely knew the first was not a firecracker and was of the opinion the shots came from behind him.[25]

Harold Elkins

Elkins was standing close to the crossroads at Main Street and Houston Street.

> I immediately ran to the area from which it sounded like the shots had been fired. This is an area between the railroads and the Texas School Book Depository which is east of the railroads.[26]

Ronald Fischer

Fischer was standing on the southwest corner of the crossroads at Houston Street and Elm Street, just opposite the TSBD.

> **Mr Belin** : Where did the shots appear to be coming from?

23. Faye Chism: *WCHE*, vol.19, p.472 (22 November 1963).
24. John Chism: *WCHE*, vol.19, p.471 (22 November 1963).
25. CE 2091 (*WCHE*, vol.24, p.525) (18 December 1963).
26. Harold Elkins: *WCHE*, vol.19, p.540 (26 November 1964).

Mr Fischer : They appeared to be coming from just west of the School Book Depository Building. There were some railroad tracks and there were some railroad cars back in there.

Mr Belin : And they appeared to be coming from those railroad cars?

Mr Fischer : Well, that area somewhere.[27]

Buell Wesley Frazier

Frazier, who had driven Oswald to work that morning, was standing on the front steps of the TSBD.

Mr Ball : Now, then, did you have any impression at that time as to the direction from which the sound came?

Mr Frazier : Well to be frank with you I thought it come from down there, you know, where that underpass is. There is a series, quite a few number of them railroad tracks running together and from where I was standing it sounded like it was coming from down the railroad tracks there.[28]

Dorothy Garner

Garner was watching the motorcade from a fourth–floor window of the TSBD.

> I thought at the time the shots or reports came from a point to the west of the building.[29]

Jean Hill

Jean Hill was standing on the south side of Elm Street, just a few yards from President Kennedy as he was shot in the head.

27. Ronald Fischer: *WCHE*, vol.6, p.195 (1 April 1964).
28. Buell Frazier: *WCHE*, vol.2, p.234 (11 March 1964).
29. Dorothy Garner: CE 1381, p.33 (*WCHE*, vol.22, p.648) (20 March 1964).

Mrs. Hill stated she heard from four to six shots in all and believes they came from a spot just west of the Texas School Book Depository Building.[30]

Mrs Hill : I didn't realize that the shots were coming from the building. I frankly thought they were coming from the knoll.

Mr Specter : Why did you think they were coming from the knoll?

Mrs Hill : That was just my idea where they were coming from.

Mr Specter : Would you draw the knoll on the picture, where you mean by the knoll?

Mrs Hill : This area in front of the Book Depository — it's right here.

Mr Specter : Just draw me a circle as to where you had a general impression the shots were coming from.

Mrs Hill : This is a hill and it was like they were coming from right in there....

Mr Specter : Now, did you have a conscious impression of the source of the first shot that you heard, that is, where it came from?

Mrs Hill : Well, evidently I didn't because the only conscious recollection I have of that ...I had always thought that they came from the knoll.... As I said, I thought they were coming from the general direction of that knoll.

...

Mr Specter : You just had the general impression that shots were coming from the knoll?

Mrs Hill : Yes.[31]

30. Jean Hill: CE 2582, p.2 (*WCHE*, vol.25, p.854) (13 March 1964).
31. *WCHE*, vol.6, pp.212–213 (24 March 1964).

S.M. Holland

Sam Holland was standing on the railway bridge known as the triple underpass, at the west end of Dealey Plaza.

> When they got just about to the Arcade I heard what I thought for the moment was a fire cracker and he slumped over and I looked over toward the arcade and trees and saw a puff of smoke come from the trees and I heard three more shots after the first shot but that was the only puff of smoke I saw.... But the puff of smoke I saw definitely came from behind the arcade through the trees.[32]

> HOLLAND stated that he looked toward the fence to his left to observe anyone that he might see running from this fence but saw no one.
>
> The only unusual thing that HOLLAND could recall was an approximate one and one–half to two foot diameter of what he believed was gray smoke which appeared to him to be coming from the trees which would have been on the right of the Presidential car but observed no one there or in the vicinity.[33]

Mr Holland : I counted four shots and about the same time all this was happening, and in this group of trees — [indicating].

Mr Stern : Now, you are indicating trees on the north side of Elm Street?

Mr Holland : These trees right along here [indicating].

Mr Stern : Let's mark this Exhibit C and draw a circle around the trees you are referring to.

Mr Holland : Right in there. [Indicating.] ...And a puff of smoke came out about 6 or 8 feet above the ground right out from under those trees. And at just about this location from where I was standing

32. S.M. Holland: *WCHE*, vol.19, p.480 (22 November 1963).
33. CD 5, pp.49–50 (24 November 1963).

you could see that puff of smoke, like someone had thrown a fire–cracker or something out, and that is just about the way it sounded.... There were definitely four reports.

Mr Stern : You have no doubt about that?

Mr Holland : I have no doubt about it. I have no doubt about seeing that puff of smoke come out from under those trees either.[34]

Ed Johnson

Ed Johnson, a reporter for the *Fort Worth Star–Telegram*, was in the press bus, a few car–lengths back in the motorcade, and described his experiences in the next day's paper:

> The shots snapped out in the brisk, clear noon air.
>
> Some reporter said, "My God, what's that? It must be shots."
>
> The caravan kept wheeling on, picking up speed.
>
> Some of the White House reporters yelled for the bus driver to stop. He kept on going, heading toward the Stemmons Expressway.
>
> Some of us saw little puffs of white smoke that seemed to hit the grassy area in the esplanade that divides Dallas' main downtown streets.[35]

Dolores Kounas

Kounas was standing on the south side of Elm Street, opposite the TSBD.

> It sounded as though these shots were coming from the Triple Underpass.... She stated it did not sound like the shots were coming from that [TSBD] direction but rather from the Triple Underpass.[36]

34. *WCHE*, vol.6, pp.243–244 (8 April 1964).
35. Ed Johnson: *Fort Worth Star–Telegram*, 23 November 1963, p.2.
36. Dolores Kounas: CE 1439 (*WCHE*, vol.22, p.846) (24 November 1963).

> Although I was across the street from the Depository building and was looking in the direction of the building as the motorcade passed and following the shots, I did not look up at the building as I had thought the shots came from a westerly direction in the vicinity of the viaduct.[37]

Paul Landis

Paul Landis was a Secret Service agent in the car immediately behind President Kennedy's car.

> My reaction at this time was that the [fatal] shot came from somewhere towards the front.[38]

Billy Lovelady

Lovelady was standing on the front steps of the TSBD. His physical similarity to Oswald led to some confusion; see Appendix E, Was Oswald Standing in the Doorway?, p.169 below.

> I heard several loud reports which I first thought to be firecrackers and which appeared to me to be in the direction of Elm Street viaduct just ahead of the Motorcade. I did not at any time believe the shots had come from the Texas School Book Depository.[39]

Mr Ball : Where was the direction of the sound?

Mr Lovelady : Right there around that concrete little deal on that knoll.

Mr Ball : That's where it sounded to you?

Mr Lovelady : Yes, sir; to my right....

Mr Ball : From the underpass area?

Mr Lovelady : Between the underpass and the building right on that knoll.[40]

37. CE 1381, p.57 (*WCHE*, vol.22, p.659) (23 March 1964).
38. Paul Landis: CE 1024 (*WCHE*, vol.18, p.759) (17 November 1963).
39. Billy Lovelady: CE 1381, p.62 (*WCHE*, vol.22, p.662) (19 March 1964).
40. *WCHE*, vol.6, p.338 (7 April 1964).

Austin Miller

Miller was standing with other railway employees on the Triple Underpass.

> I saw something which I thought was smoke or steam coming from a group of trees north of Elm off the Railroad tracks.[41]

> **Mr Belin** : Where did the shots sound like they came from?
>
> **Mr Miller** : Well, the way it sounded like, it came from the, I would say from right there in the car. Would be to my left, the way I was looking at him over toward that incline.[42]

A.J. Millican

> I was standing on the North side of Elm Street, about half way between Houston and the Underpass.... I heard three shots come from up toward Houston and Elm right by the Book Depository Building, and then immediately I heard two more shots come from the Arcade between the Book Store and the Underpass, and then three more shots came from the same direction only sounded further back.[43]

Luke Mooney

Mooney, a deputy sheriff, was standing on Main Street, on the edge of Dealey Plaza. He was one of the officers who found the rifle hidden under boxes on the sixth floor.

> **Mr Ball** : Why did you go over to the railroad yard?

41. Austin Miller: *WCHE*, vol.19, p.485 (22 November 1963).
42. *WCHE*, vol.6, p.225 (8 April 1964).
43. A.J. Millican: *WCHE*, vol.19, p.486 (no date, but filed with a group of similar statements given on 22 November 1963).

> **Mr Mooney** : Well, that was — from the echo of the shots, we thought they came from that direction.[44]

Thomas Murphy

Murphy was standing on the Triple Underpass.

> MURPHY said in his opinion these shots came from a spot just west of the Texas School Book Depository Building.[45]

Jean Newman

Jean Newman was standing on the north side of Elm Street, between the TSBD and the knoll.

> The first impression I had was that the shots came from my right.[46]

> She stated that when she realized the reports were shots she immediately turned and looked up the hill to the North toward the parking lot but did not see anything.[47]

William Newman

William Newman (no relation to Jean Newman) was also standing on the north side of Elm Street, a little further along toward the knoll.

> I thought the shot had come from the garden directly behind me, that was on an elevation from where I was as I was right on the curb. I do not recall looking toward the Texas School Book Depository. I looked back in the vacinity [*sic*] of the garden.[48]

44. Luke Mooney: *WCHE*, vol.3, p.283 (25 March 1964).
45. Thomas Murphy: CE 1439 (*WCHE*, vol.22, p.835) (17 March 1964).
46. Jean Newman: *WCHE*, vol.19, p.489 (22 November 1963).
47. CE 1439 (*WCHE*, vol.22, p.843) (24 November 1963).
48. William Newman: *WCHE*, vol.19, p.490 (22 November 1963).

Kenneth O'Donnell and David Powers

Two members of the White House staff, Kenneth O'Donnell and David Powers, were travelling in the Secret Service car immediately behind President Kennedy's car. O'Donnell testified that the shots came from the rear.[49] Powers agreed, but added that "I also had a fleeting impression that the noise appeared to come from the front in the area of the triple overpass."[50]

The politician, Tip O'Neill, claimed in his memoirs that both men had in fact heard shots from the grassy knoll:

> I was never one of those people who had doubts or suspicions about the Warren Commission's report on the president's death. But five years after Jack died, I was having dinner with Kenny O'Donnell and a few other people at Jimmy's Harborside Restaurant in Boston, and we got to talking about the assassination.
>
> I was surprised to hear O'Donnell say that he was sure he had heard two shots that came from behind the fence.
>
> "That's not what you told the Warren Commission," I said.
>
> "You're right, " he replied. "I told the FBI what I had heard, but they said it couldn't have happened that way and that I must have been imagining things. So I testified the way they wanted me to. I just didn't want to stir up any more pain and trouble for the family."
>
> "I can't believe it," I said. "I wouldn't have done that in a million years. I would have told them the truth."
>
> "Tip, you have to understand. The family — everybody wanted this thing behind them."
>
> Dave Powers was with us at dinner that night, and his recollection of the shots was the same as O'Donnell's. Kenny O'Donnell is no longer alive, but during the

49. Kenneth O'Donnell: *WCHE*, vol.7, p.448.
50. David Powers: *ibid.*, p.473.

writing of this book I checked with Dave Powers. As they say in the news business, he stands by his story.[51]

Roberta Parker

Parker was standing directly opposite the main entrance to the TSBD.

> The shot sounded to her as though it had come from a cement memorial building to the north of the Texas School Book Depository on Elm Street. She looked in that direction but saw nothing that she could relate to the shot. During this time, she heard two additional shots and in looking around, glanced at the Texas School Book Depository building which was directly across Elm from her.[52]

Frank Reilly

Reilly was standing with other railway workers on the railway bridge at the west end of Dealey Plaza.

> He saw two cars turn on Elm toward the underpass and at this time heard three shots which he thought came from the trees west of the Texas School Book Depository.[53]

> **Mr Ball** : What did you hear?
>
> **Mr Reilly** : Three shots.
>
> **Mr Ball** : Where did they seem to come from; what direction?
>
> **Mr Reilly** : It seemed to me like they come out of the trees.
>
> **Mr Ball** : What trees?

51. Thomas P. O'Neill, Jr., *Man of the House: The Life and Political Memoirs of Speaker Tip O'Neill*, Random House, 1987, p.178.
52. Roberta Parker: CD 205, p.504 (16 December 1963).
53. Frank Reilly: *ibid.*, p.29 (18 December 1963).

Mr Reilly : On the north side of Elm Street at the corner up there.

Mr Ball : On the north side of Elm — on what corner?

Mr Reilly : Well, where all those trees are — you've never been down there?

Mr Ball : Yes: I've been there, but you tell me — I want you to tell me because it has to go on the record here and it has to be in writing.

Mr Reilly : Well, it's at that park where all the shrubs is up there — it's to the north of Elm Street — up the slope.[54]

Arnold Rowland

Arnold Rowland was standing on the east side of Houston Street, facing the TSBD.

Mr Specter : Did you have any impression or reaction as to the point of origin when you heard the first noise?

Mr Rowland : Well, I began looking, I didn't look at the building mainly, and as practically any of the police officers there will tell you, the echo effect was such that it sounded like it came from the railroad yards. That is where I looked, that is where all the policemen, everyone, converged on the railroads.

...

Mr Specter : Now, as to the second shot, did you have any impression as to the point of origin or source?

Mr Rowland : The same point or very close to it.

Mr Specter : And how about the third shot?

Mr Rowland : Very close to the same position.

...

54. *WCHE*, vol.6, p.230 (8 April 1964).

Mr Specter : After the shots occurred, did you ever look back at the Texas School Book Depository Building?

Mr Rowland : No; I did not. In fact, I went over toward the scene of the railroad yards myself.

Mr Specter : Why did you not look back at the Texas School Book Depository Building in view of the fact that you had seen a man with a rifle up there earlier in the day?

Mr Rowland : I don't remember. It was mostly due to the confusion, and then the fact that it sounded like it came from this area "C", and that all the officers, enforcement officers, were converging on that area, and I just didn't pay any attention to it at that time.[55]

Edgar Smith

Edgar Smith, a police officer, was standing on Houston Street, near the junction with Elm Street.

Mr Smith : I thought when it came to my mind that there were shots, and I was pretty sure there were when I saw his car because they were leaving in such a hurry, I thought they were coming from this area here, and I ran over there and back of it and, of course, there wasn't anything there.

Mr Liebeler : You thought the shot came from this little concrete structure up behind No. 7?

Mr Smith : Yes, sir.

Mr Liebeler : On Commission Exhibit 354?

Mr Smith : Yes.

Mr Liebeler : Toward the railroad tracks there?

Mr Smith : That's true.[56]

55. Arnold Rowland: *WCHE*, vol.2, pp.180–181 (10 March 1964).
56. Edgar Smith: *WCHE*, vol.7, p.568 (24 July 1964). CE 354: *WCHE*, vol.16, p.949.

Joe Marshall Smith

Like his fellow police officer, Edgar Smith, Joe Marshall Smith (no relation) was at the corner of Elm Street and Houston Street.

> [T]he reporter calling stated he had interviewed Patrolman J. M. Smith who advised that he definitely distinguished the aroma of gunpowder near the underpass.... He stated he did smell what he thought was gunpowder but stated this smell was in the parking lot by the TSBD Building and not by the underpass. He advised he never at any time went to the underpass and could not advise if there was the smell of gunpowder in the underpass.[57]

> I heard the shots and thought they were coming from bushes of the overpass.[58]

> **Mr Liebeler** : Did you have any basis for believing where the shots came from, or where to look for somebody, other than what the lady told you?
>
> **Mr Smith** : No, sir; except that maybe it was a power of suggestion. But it sounded to me like they may have came from this vicinity here.
>
> **Mr Liebeler** : Down around the — let's put a No. 5 there [on Commission Exhibit 354] at the corner here behind this concrete structure where the bushes were down toward the railroad tracks from the Texas School Book Depository Building.
>
> **Mr Smith** : Yes.
>
> **Mr Liebeler** : Now you say that you had the idea that the shots may have come from up in that area?
>
> **Mr Smith** : Yes, sir; that is just what, well, like I say, the sound of it.[59]

57. Joe Marshall Smith: CD 205, p.39 (9 December 1963).
58. CE 1358 (*WCHE*, vol.22, p.600) (16 July 1964).
59. *WCHE*, vol.7, pp.535–536 (23 July 1964).

Forrest Sorrels

Forrest Sorrels, a Secret Service agent, was in the car immediately following the presidential car.

> I looked towards the top of the terrace to my right as the sound of the shots seemed to come from that direction.[60]

James Tague

James Tague, the third man wounded in Dealey Plaza, was standing close to the point where Commerce Street meets Main Street, by the triple underpass.

> **Mr Liebeler** : Did you have any idea where these shots came from when you heard them ringing out?
>
> **Mr Tague** : Yes; I thought they were coming from my left.
>
> **Mr Liebeler** : Immediately to your left, or toward the back? Of course, now we have other evidence that would indicate that the shots did come from the Texas School Book Depository, but see if we can disregard that and determine just what you heard when the shots were fired in the first place.
>
> **Mr Tague** : To recall everything is almost impossible. Just an impression is all I recall, is the fact that my first impression was that up by the, whatever you call the monument, or whatever it was —
>
> . . .
>
> **Mr Liebeler** : Your impression of where the shots came from was much the result of the activity near No. 7 [on Commission Exhibit 354]?
>
> **Mr Tague** : Not when I heard the shots.
>
> **Mr Liebeler** : You thought they had come from the area between Nos. 7 and 5?

60. Forrest Sorrels: *WCHE*, vol.21, p.548 (28 November 1963).

Mr Tague : I believe they came from up in here.

Mr Liebeler : Back in the area "C"?

Mr Tague : Right.

Mr Liebeler : Behind the concrete monument here between Nos. 7 and 5, toward the general area of "C"?

Mr Tague : Yes.[61]

Roy Truly

Roy Truly, a director and the superintendant of the Texas School Book Depository, was standing with Ochus Campbell on the north side of Elm Street, close to the TSBD. Shortly afterwards, he encountered Lee Oswald in the canteen on the second floor of the TSBD.

Mr Belin : Where did you think the shots came from?

Mr Truly : I thought the shots came from the vicinity of the railroad or the WPA project, behind the WPA project west of the building.[62]

Harry Weatherford

Weatherford, a deputy sheriff, was standing outside the Criminal Court building on Main Street.

> I heard a loud report which I thought was a railroad torpedo, as it sounded as if it came from the railroad yard. Thinking, this was a heck of a time for one to go off, then I heard a 2nd report which had more of an echo report and thought to myself, that this was a rifle and I started towards the corner when I heard the 3rd report. By this time I was running towards the railroad yards where the sound seemed to come from.[63]

61. James Tague: *WCHE*, vol.7, pp.556–557 (23 March 1964).
62. Roy Truly: *WCHE*, vol.3, p.227 (24 March 1964). The 'WPA project' is the concrete pergola, built by the Works Projects Administration.
63. Harry Weatherford: *WCHE*, vol.19, p.502 (23 November 1963).

Seymour Weitzman

Weitzman was one of the law officers who discovered the rifle on the sixth floor of the TSBD. At the time of the shooting, he was on the corner of Main Street and Houston Street.

> I ran in a northwest direction and scaled a fence towards where we thought the shots came from.[64]

Otis Williams

Williams was standing on the front steps of the TSBD.

> Just after the Presidential car passed the building and went out of sight over the Elm Street embankment I heard three loud blasts. I thought these blasts or shots came from the direction of the viaduct which crosses Elm Street.[65]

Mary Woodward

Mary Woodward, a journalist on the *Dallas Morning News*, was standing on the north side of Elm Street, about halfway between the TSBD and the grassy knoll. She wrote about her experience in the following day's paper.

> Suddenly there was a horrible, ear–shattering noise coming from behind us and a little to the right.[66]

> United States Attorney H. BAREFOOT SANDERS, Dallas, Texas, telephonically advised ASAC KYLE G. CLARK on December 5, 1963, that a reporter for the Dallas "Morning News", name unrecalled, had advised him that four of the women working in the Society Section

64. Seymour Weitzman: CE 2003, p.63 (*WCHE*, vol.24, p.228) (23 November 1963).
65. Otis Williams: CE 1381, p.105 (*WCHE*, vol.22, p.683) (19 March 1964).
66. Mary Woodward, 'Witness From the News Describes Assassination,' *Dallas Morning News*, 23 November 1963, p.3.

> of the Dallas "Morning News" were reportedly standing next to Mr. ZAPRUDA [*sic*] when the assassination shots were fired. According to this reporter, these women, names unknown, stated that the shots according to their opinion came from a direction other than from the Texas School Book Depository (TSBD) Building.[67]

> She stated that her first reaction was that the shots had been fired from above her head and from possibly behind her. Her next reaction was that the shots might have come from the overpass which was to her right. She stated, however, because of the loud echo, she could not say where the shots had come from, other than they had come from above her head.[68]

Abraham Zapruder

Abraham Zapruder famously filmed the assassination from the top of a concrete pedestal on Elm Street close to the grassy knoll.

> According to Mr. Zapruder, the position of the assassin was behind Mr. Zapruder.[69]

> **Mr Zapruder** : I remember the police were running behind me. There were police running right behind me. Of course, they didn't realize yet, I guess, where the shot came from — that it came from that height.
>
> **Mr Liebeler** : As you were standing on this abutment facing Elm street, you say the police ran over behind the concrete structure behind you and down the railroad track behind that, is that right?
>
> **Mr Zapruder** : After the shots?
>
> **Mr Liebeler** : Yes.

67. CD 205, p.39. ASAC stands for Assistant Special Agent in Charge: the FBI agent who is second in command of a local office.
68. CE 2084 (*WCHE*, vol.24, p.520) (6 December 1963).
69. Abraham Zapruder: CD 87 (22 November 1963).

Mr Zapruder : Yes — after the shots — yes, some of them were motorcycle cops – I guess they left their motorcycles running and they were running right behind me, of course, in the line of the shooting. I guess they thought it came from right behind me.

Mr Liebeler : Did you have any impression as to the direction from which these shots came?

Mr Zapruder : No, I also thought it came from back of me. Of course, you can't tell when something is in line — it could come from anywhere, but being I was here and he was hit on this line and he was hit right in the head — I saw it right around here, so it looked like it came from here and it could come from there.

Mr Liebeler : All right, as you stood here on the abutment and looked down into Elm Street, you saw the President hit on the right side of the head and you thought perhaps the shots had come from behind you?

Mr Zapruder : Well, yes.[70]

Other Witnesses

A few witnesses made statements more ambiguous than those quoted above, that could be interpreted as supporting one or more shots from the grassy knoll:

Eugene Boone

> I heard three shots coming from the vicinity of where the President's car was.[71]

E.V. Brown

> he believed he could smell gunpowder in the air on the overpass.[72]

70. *WCHE*, vol.7, pp.571–572 (22 July 1964).
71. Eugene Boone: *WCHE*, vol.19, p.508 (22 November 1963).
72. E.V. Brown: CD 205, pp.39–40 (9 December 1963).

James Crawford

> the sound, I thought it was a backfire in the cavalcade from down the hill, down the hill toward the underpass.[73]

Avery Davis

> I did not know from which direction the shots had come, but thought they were from the direction of the viaduct which crosses Elm Street west from where I was standing.[74]

Emmett Hudson

> The shots that I heard definately [*sic*] came from behind and above me.[75]

Clemon Johnson

> white smoke was observed near the pavillion, [*sic*] but he felt that this smoke came from a motorcycle abandoned near the spot by a Dallas policeman.[76]

Joe Molina

> sort of kind of came from the west side.[77]

Samuel Paternostro

> heard a report or shot which he believed came from the Texas School Book Depository (TSBD) building or the Criminal Courts Building or the triple overpass.[78]

73. James Crawford: *WCHE*, vol.6, p.173 (1 April 1964).
74. Avery Davis: CE 1381, p.22 (*WCHE*, vol.22, p.642) (20 March 1964).
75. Emmett Hudson: *WCHE*, vol.19, p.481 (22 November 1963); *cf*. CD 205, p.30 and *HSCA Report*, pp.605–606.
76. Clemon Johnson: CE 1422 (*WCHE*, vol.22, p.836) (18 March 1964).
77. Joe Molina: *WCHE*, vol.6, p.371 (7 April 1964).
78. Samuel Paternostro: CE 2106 (*WCHE*, vol.24, p.536) (20 January 1964).

Nolan Potter

he recalls seeing smoke in front of the Texas School Book Depository Building rising above the trees.[79]

Jesse Price

he assumed the shot had come from the overpass.[80]

Madie Reese

At first she thought the shots came from the alcove near the benches.[81]

William Shelley

Sounded like it came from the west.[82]

James Simmons

he thought he saw exhaust fumes of smoke near the embankment in front of the Texas School Book Depository Building.[83]

Garland Slack

the sound as he first heard it seemed to come from the direction of the overpass.[84]

Steven Wilson

At the time it seemed the shots came from the west end of the building or from the colonnade located on Elm Street across from the west end of our building. The

79. Nolan Potter: CE 1418 (*WCHE*, vol.22, p.834) (19 March 1964).
80. Jesse Price: CD 205, p.65 (25 November 1963).
81. Madie Reese: CD 205, p.59 (24 November 1963).
82. William Shelley: *WCHE*, vol.6, p.329 (7 April 1964).
83. James Simmons: CE 1416 (*WCHE*, vol.22, p.833) (19 March 1964).
84. Garland Slack: CE 2909 (*WCHE*, vol.26, p.364) (2 December 1963).

shots really did not sound like they came from above me.[85]

Disputed Witnesses

Not all of the following witnesses are equally credible, but they all crop up in various accounts of the assassination.

Gordon Arnold

In 1978, the *Dallas Morning News* reported the claims of Gordon Arnold to have witnessed the assassination. Arnold, a soldier on leave, had apparently been standing close to the fence on the grassy knoll when he encountered a man who brandished Secret Service credentials. On hearing shots from behind the fence, Arnold fell to the ground. Although the existence of the apparently bogus Secret Service agent had been mentioned 15 years earlier by witnesses such as Joe Marshall Smith and Seymour Weitzman,[86] there is no conclusive evidence that Arnold himself was actually in Dealey Plaza during the assassination. He is not visible in any photographs or films, and none of the witnesses in the vicinity of the knoll mention his presence. He did, however, receive some support from Senator Ralph Yarborough, who was riding in the motorcade. Yarborough contacted the journalist Earl Golz, who had made Arnold's story public, and told Golz that he had seen a man fall to the ground in the way Arnold had described. Yarborough may have seen Arnold, or he may instead have seen William Newman, who certainly fell to the ground close to the grassy knoll immediately after the fatal shot.[87]

85. Steven Wilson: CE 1381, p.107 (*WCHE*, vol.22, p.685) (25 March 1964).
86. J.M. Smith: *WCHE*, vol.7, pp.535–536. Seymour Weitzman: *WCHE*, vol.7, p.107.
87. For more about Arnold's story, see: Earl Golz, 'SS Imposters Spotted by JFK Witnesses,' *Dallas Morning News*, 27 August 1978, p.1A; James Douglass, *JFK and the Unspeakable: Why He Died and Why It Matters*, Orbis Books, 2008, pp.261–262; and Henry Hurt, *Reasonable Doubt: An Investigation into the Assassination of John F. Kennedy*, Henry Holt, 1985, pp.111–113.

Cheryl McKinnon

Another possible witness whose presence in Dealey Plaza cannot be substantiated is Cheryl McKinnon, a journalism student who claimed to have been standing on the north side of Elm Street. Cheryl McKinnon does not appear to have offered an opinion on the source of the shots, or indeed on the assassination itself, until 20 years afterwards, when she wrote an account of her experiences for a newspaper:

> On Nov. 22, 1963, I stood, along with hundreds of others, on the grassy knoll in Dealey Plaza....
>
> As we stood watching the motorcade turn onto Elm Street, I tried to grasp every tiny detail of both President and Mrs Kennedy, "How happy they look," I thought. Suddenly, three shots in rapid succession rang out. Myself and dozens of others standing nearby turned in horror toward the back of the grassy knoll where it seemed the sounds had originated. Puffs of white smoke still hung in the air in small patches. But no one was visible....
>
> I have read the Warren Commission Report in its entirety and dozens of other books as well. I am sorry to say that the only thing I am absolutely sure of today is that at least two of the shots fired that day in Dealey Plaza came from behind where I stood on the knoll, not from the book depository.[88]

Doris Mumford

Cheryl McKinnon is frequently identified, without any supporting evidence, as the woman wearing sunglasses who is seen in several films and photographs, crouching on the grass. The woman in question has also been identified by Karen Moore, a contributor to an online forum, as her mother, Doris Mumford.[89] Photographs uploaded to the forum are consistent with the identification of the

88. Cheryl McKinnon: *San Diego Star–News*, 22 November 1983.
89. Doris Mumford: http://www.jfkassassinationforum.com/index.php/topic,8837.0.html.

woman as Doris Mumford, who at the time of the assassination was 36 years old and living in Richardson, a few miles north of Dallas. In a comment on the jfkfacts.org blog, Karen Moore writes that her mother was standing near William Newman, and "heard three shots, they came from behind her, and she saw the life leave the President's face."[90]

Lee Bowers

Lee Bowers was working in the railway control tower north of the car park at the top of the grassy knoll. He was not sure where the sound of the shots came from:

> **Mr Ball** : And were you able to form an opinion as to the source of the sound or what direction it came from, I mean?
>
> **Mr Bowers** : The sounds came either from up against the School Depository Building or near the mouth of the triple underpass.
>
> **Mr Ball** : Were you able to tell which?
>
> **Mr Bowers** : No, I could not.[91]

Bowers did, however, testify to having seen unusual activity behind the fence on the grassy knoll. A few minutes before the assassination, three unfamiliar cars came into the car park, drove around, and left. One of the drivers appeared to be using a walkie–talkie. More significantly, Bowers appears to claim that two men were standing behind the fence:

> **Mr Ball** : Now, were there any people standing on the high side — high ground between your tower and where Elm Street goes down under the underpass toward the mouth of the underpass?
>
> **Mr Bowers** : Directly in line, towards the mouth of the underpass, there were two men. One man,

90. http://jfkfacts.org/assassination/fact-check/credible-witness-bill-newmans-story/.
91. Lee Bowers: *WCHE*, vol.6, p.287 (2 April 1964).

middle–aged, or slightly older, fairly heavy–set, in a white shirt, fairly dark trousers. Another younger man, about midtwenties, in either a plaid shirt or plaid coat or jacket.

Mr Ball : Were they standing together or standing separately?

Mr Bowers : They were standing within 10 or 15 feet of each other, and gave no appearance of being together, as far as I knew.

Mr Ball : In what direction were they facing?

Mr Bowers : They were facing and looking up towards Main and Houston, and following the caravan as it came down.

...

Mr Ball : Did you see any activity in this high ground above Elm after the shot?

Mr Bowers : At the time of the shooting there seemed to be some commotion....

Mr Ball : When you said there was a commotion, what do you mean by that? What did it look like to you when you were looking at the commotion?

Mr Bowers : I just am unable to describe rather than it was something out of the ordinary, a sort of milling around, but something occurred in this particular spot which was out of the ordinary, which attracted my eye for some reason, which I could not identify.

Mr Ball : You couldn't describe it?

Mr Bowers : Nothing that I could pinpoint as having happened that —

Mr Ball : Afterwards did a good many people come up there on this high ground at the tower?[92]

And so Joseph Ball changed the subject. Bowers did not supply explicit evidence to the authorities of gunshots from the grassy

92. *Ibid.*, pp.287–288.

knoll, but his credible account of two men standing by the fence, and of a 'commotion' at the time of the shooting, surely makes him one of the most intriguing eye–witnesses to the assassination.

Shortly before his untimely death in a car crash in 1966, Lee Bowers was interviewed for Mark Lane's film, *Rush to Judgment*. Extracts from the interview can be found online. According to a transcript of the interview, Bowers suggests that the two men he saw may have been on the steps leading up from Elm Street, rather than behind the fence: "And one of them, from time to time as he walked back and forth, er, disappeared behind a wooden fence which also is slightly to the west of that." Bowers does, however, give a more detailed description of the 'commotion':

> At the time of the shooting, in the vicinity of where the two men I have described were, there was a flash of light or, as far as I am concerned, something I could not identify, but there was something which occurred which caught my eye in this immediate area on the embankment. Now, what this was, I could not state at that time and at the time I could not identify it, other than there was some unusual occurrence — a flash of light or smoke or something which caused me to feel like something out of the ordinary had occurred there.

Ed Hoffman

Ed Hoffman, who was deaf, was standing on Stemmons Freeway, about 200 yards to the west of Dealey Plaza. He claimed to have seen two men in the railway yard behind the fence on the grassy knoll, followed by a puff of smoke among the trees, and finally one of the men passing a rifle to the other, who disassembled it, packed it in a bag, and made his escape while the first man went back to the fence.[93]

93. For details of Hoffman's account, see: Douglass, *op. cit.*, pp.262–266; Ed Hoffman with Ron Friedrich, *Eye Witness*, JFK Lancer, 1997; Ron Friedrich, 'Ed Hoffman's Changing Story,' *Kennedy Assassination Chronicles*, vol.1 issue 2 (June 1995), pp.31–32, which argues that the apparent inconsistencies in Hoffman's story are due to his interviewers' unfamiliarity with American Sign Language; and M. Duke Lane, 'Freeway Man,' at http://mcadams.posc.mu.edu/freewayman.htm, which argues strongly that Hoffman's story was largely invented, albeit for understandable reasons.

D Is the Zapruder Film Authentic?

One of the more regrettable trends in discussions of the JFK assassination is the willingness of some commentators to dispose of inconvenient items of evidence by alleging that they have been manipulated or faked. From about the mid–1980s, allegations appeared that the Zapruder film had been altered. Theories range from the just–about–plausible, though as yet unsubstantiated, idea that a patch was applied to a tiny area on a handful of frames in order to conceal evidence of damage to the back of President Kennedy's head, to the outrageously implausible idea that the entire film is a fabrication.[1]

Several pieces of documentary evidence in the JFK assassination do appear to have been altered or forged, but there is currently no good reason to suppose that the Zapruder film is one of them.[2] There are five grounds for believing the film to be genuine. Firstly, the film's chain of possession is well documented, and provides no opportunity for conspirators to have gained access to the film before it had been copied and those copies had been widely distributed. Abraham Zapruder had the film in his possession from

1. For a representative sample of the case for alteration, see Philip Melanson, 'Hidden Exposure: Cover–Up and Intrigue in the CIA: Secret Possession of the Zapruder Film,' *The Third Decade*, vol.1 no.1 (November 1984), pp.13–21; and James Fetzer, ed., *The Great Zapruder Film Hoax: Deceit and Deception in the Death of JFK*, Catfeet Press, 2003.

2. If, as the balance of the evidence indicates, Lee Harvey Oswald did not fire a rifle during the assassination, several pieces of evidence must be fraudulent: the rifle that had been discovered on the sixth floor of the Texas School Book Depository; the bullet shells associated with it; and Commission Exhibit 399, which appears to have been entered into evidence fraudulently, as does the paper bag supposedly discovered on the sixth floor.

the time of the assassination until 11 o'clock that night, when he was telephoned at home by Richard Stolley of *Life* magazine, and then again at 8 o'clock the next morning, when he brought the film with him to his office. As David Wrone, the author of the definitive study of the film, points out:

> Conspirators would have had to enter Zapruder's home, locate the film, steal it, whisk it to the airport, and fly it to Washington in an almost three–hour flight. Then another team would have had to meet the plane, take the film, and speed it to a laboratory, where yet another team altered the frames, no easy task to say the least.

The conspirators would have had to repeat this process in reverse to place the new film in the possession of Zapruder, who failed to notice either of the two necessary break–ins at his home. Wrone concludes that transportation and processing alone, not including the actual alteration of the film, required that "at least ten hours would be consumed — that is, the film could not have been returned until at least three hours after it had been shown and sold in Zapruder's office, an impossibility that renders the allegation false."[3]

Secondly, there are no obvious contradictions between the Zapruder film and the rest of the photographic evidence, including the three other home movies that depict the shooting. Any photograph or film could have contained clear evidence that the Zapruder film had been altered, but no unambiguous examples of inconsistencies have yet been demonstrated. Several have been proposed, but there are straightforward explanations for all of them: they are either the by–products of poor–quality photographic reproductions, or the result of wishful thinking. Hundreds of photographs and several home movies recorded various aspects of the

3. David Wrone, *The Zapruder Film: Reframing JFK's Assassination*, University Press of Kansas, 2003, pp.124–125. The authenticity of the Zapruder film is also defended by Josiah Thompson, 'Bedrock Evidence in the Kennedy Assassination,' at http://www.maryferrell.org/mffweb/archive/viewer/showDoc.do?docId=11957. For a technical account of the authenticity of the original film and the copies in the National Archives, see Roland Zavada, *Analysis of Selected Motion Picture Photographic Evidence*, Kodak Technical Report, Eastman Kodak, 1998.

motorcade's progress through Dealey Plaza. They form a consistent body of evidence.[4]

Thirdly, it would not have been possible to be certain that all such contradictions had been eliminated. Conspirators did not have access to the whole of the photographic evidence, and thus could not have known whether any alterations to the Zapruder film were at risk of being revealed. Nor could they have known how many photographs and other movies would consequently have needed to be altered to make them consistent with the forged Zapruder film. The investigating authorities made little effort to identify photographers or to obtain photographs and movies, many of which were not made public until long after the assassination. Some images may still remain hidden, such as those from an unidentified woman who appears to have been pointing a still or movie camera directly at President Kennedy as he was shot in the head, just a few yards in front of her.

Fourthly, altering the film would have been a very inefficient way of concealing the evidence contained within it. The Zapruder film was one of the few items of photographic material that came to the attention of the authorities very soon after the assassination. Rather than take on the almost impossible task of altering the film, it would have been far easier simply to seize the film and make it disappear.

Finally, the most powerful and obvious point: the Zapruder film can hardly have been altered to cover up evidence of conspiracy, given that it contains almost irrefutable evidence of conspiracy. When combined with certain uncontroversial facts, the Zapruder film provides explicit disproof of the single–bullet theory: Kennedy's reaction to his throat wound occurs earlier than Connally's reaction to his back wound, which in turn occurs earlier than Connally's wrist wound. Famously, the film also reveals Kennedy's sharp back–and–to–the–left movement in reaction to what can only plausibly be interpreted as a shot from in front. If anyone did manage to alter the Zapruder film, they didn't make a very good job of it.

As well as claims of discrepancies between the Zapruder film

4. For a survey of the wide range of photographs and films taken during the assassination, see Richard Trask, *Pictures of the Pain: Photography and the Assassination of President Kennedy*, Yeoman Press, 1994.

and the rest of the photographic evidence, other allegations have been made. One of the more far–fetched arguments for alteration is the discrepancy between the existing Zapruder film and an alternative version, which a handful of assassination researchers claim to have seen. This 'other' film is supposed to contain several elements that are not present on the familiar version. It is difficult to imagine how such a film, the existence of which has been reported in several parts of the world, could be accessible only to a small number of well–connected enthusiasts. The film would surely either be locked away, well out of the reach of the curious, or it would be in public circulation. As with claims of sightings of UFOs and the Loch Ness monster, we might reasonably expect conclusive physical evidence to exist. The absence of such evidence to support these claims renders them invalid. The most charitable explanation is that what the researchers saw was one or more of the many reconstructions that were filmed by official investigators and by commercial projects such as Oliver Stone's movie, *JFK*.

The strongest evidence for alteration is the discrepancy between, on the one hand, the many eye–witnesses who testified that the presidential limousine stopped on Elm Street at around the time of the fatal head shot, and, on the other hand, the Zapruder film, which shows the car slowing down but not stopping. The purpose of this particular alteration is supposed to be to cover up the complicity of the driver, a Secret Service agent. As with all cases of apparent discrepancies between physical evidence and eye–witness evidence, a more reasonable explanation is that the witnesses were simply mistaken. This is especially the case here, considering: the serious practical difficulties any forgers would have faced; the film's consistency with the rest of the photographic evidence; the fact that the car was moving directly away from most of the witnesses rather than past them, thereby making its speed more difficult to judge; and the fact that the car was closely followed by the Secret Service car, which partially obscured it from most of the spectators. Other aspects of the case show that large numbers of witnesses can indeed be mistaken. Many witnesses claimed to have heard only one, two or three shots, which cannot plausibly be true if the assassination was the result of a conspiracy; and many claimed to have heard or seen evidence of shots from the grassy knoll area, which cannot be true if the assassination was not the result of a conspiracy. At least one group must be wrong.

Once it is acknowledged that a conspiracy took place, and that some evidence had been faked, such as the planting of the rifle and the bullet shells on the sixth floor of the Texas School Book Depository, it can be tempting to suppose that any of the physical evidence might have been faked. But it is still necessary to demonstrate how a particular instance of deception might plausibly have been achieved.

For example, the planting of the evidence on the sixth floor is not in itself implausible. The TSBD was occupied by several companies, not all of whose employees would have been able to identify strangers within the building. A large majority of the 70 or more employees were not inside the building at the time of the assassination. The presence of strangers would not have been noteworthy: it was common for delivery drivers, customers, and other non–employees to enter and leave the TSBD without hindrance. The building had several rear entrances that were unlocked and unguarded. All of these entrances were close to two elevators and a set of stairs, each of which went at least as high as the sixth floor.[5]

Although fraud in the medical evidence has not yet been proved, the alteration of some of the autopsy photographs cannot be ruled out in principle, since any conspirators would have controlled all of the relevant photographic evidence, and would have had ample time in which to perform any alterations. For similar reasons, it is hardly unknown for investigating authorities to tamper with witness statements, as appears to have happened in the Oswald case.[6]

On the other hand, the physical alteration of either the Zapruder film or Kennedy's corpse would have had to be done within an infeasibly short period of time, and with incomplete access to

5. For the presence of strangers, see CE 1381, pp.5–6 (*WCHE*, vol.22, p.634). At least two of the rear entrances were open, according to Oswald's colleague, James Jarman: NARA RIF no. 180–10131–10066. For a plan of the first (i.e. ground) floor, see *WR*, p.148 (CE 1061). A detailed plan of the first floor is available online at the website of Baylor University, Poage Library, Robert Cutler Collection at http://digitalcollections.baylor.edu/cdm/ref/collection/po-jfkgkgaz/id/1263.

6. E.g. Victoria Adams, a witness whose actions immediately after the assassination imply that Oswald had not been on the sixth floor of the TSBD; see Barry Ernest, *The Girl on the Stairs: My Search for a Missing Witness to the Assassination of John F. Kennedy*, Createspace, 2011, p.106.

all the information that would have been needed to avoid detection in the future.

The current state of the evidence does not justify the conclusion that the Zapruder film is a forgery. New evidence may, of course, emerge that will provide such justification. At the moment, however, that conclusion is the result of irrational thinking. It is irrational to invent a conspiracy to explain every apparent discrepancy in the evidence. Not every such discrepancy even requires a specific explanation. Eye–witnesses can be mistaken, technical data can be incompetently assembled and analysed, and photographs can display unexpected visual effects. In any complex set of evidence, there are likely to be elements that do not match. The desire to explain everything, whether in order to find an elusive smoking gun or to stake one's claim to a particular area of study, is a harmful characteristic of much JFK assassination research. It has led to cult–like behaviour, in which anyone who fails to agree with every aspect of a particular explanation is damned as a heretic.

'Conspiracy theorist,' when used as a derogatory term, usually refers to someone for whom a conspiracy is the default explanation for events, or at least someone who uses conspiratorial explanations for events when the evidence does not justify it. That definition applies to those who, on the current state of the evidence, conclude that the Zapruder film was forged.

As a general rule, conspiracies very rarely happen. In some types of event, such as the assassinations of political figures, conspiracies are not uncommon. In the case of President Kennedy's assassination, it is almost certain that a conspiracy of some sort took place. The important question is to define the extent of that conspiracy. The fewer people and institutions that are required to be involved in a conspiracy, the more credible that conspiracy theory is. In the absence of irrefutable evidence in their favour, theories that propose the alteration of the Zapruder film, or of the president's corpse, expand the JFK conspiracy beyond reasonable limits.

Such theories are actively harmful in several ways. They divert effort from areas that may produce genuine results. They oblige rational critics of the official explanation to deal with two sets of arguments: the lone–nut arguments and the paranoid theorists' arguments. They are useful to the print and broadcast media, which defend established institutions by claiming that the lone–nut explanation is more reasonable than the alternative: "OK, so there are lots of holes in the case against Oswald, but you should see some of the stuff *those* guys are saying."

The last of these may be the most serious problem. The media gives little coverage to rational criticism of the official explanation, and tends to portray the JFK assassination debate as a simple conflict between the lone–assassin hypothesis and outrageously impractical, almost paranoid conspiracy theories. The media recognises that any reasonable alternative to the lone–assassin hypothesis implies criticism of established political institutions, and indeed of established media institutions. Consequently, it often treats the assassination in much the same way as it treats other forms of political dissent. Just as the media's coverage of demonstrations tends to concentrate on the handful of idiots or *agents provocateurs* who throw bricks through windows, so criticism of the Oswald–did–it theory is often represented by its least credible proponents. In both cases, little publicity is given to rational, critical ideas.

The similarity in each case extends to the target audience. The media's misrepresentation of the JFK assassination is not aimed primarily at those who are interested in the subject and are predisposed to think critically. Such people will hardly be prevented from discovering the large amount of informed criticism that is widely available. Nor is it aimed at those who are inclined to identify with established authority; they are unlikely to look for critical ideas, or be persuaded by any they stumble upon. It is certainly not aimed at the small number of credulous people who are liable to be taken in by the more unbelievable conspiracy theories, such as the theory that the Zapruder film was faked.

Instead, the media's message is mostly aimed at the much larger number of rational people who are aware that there is a controversy about the causes of President Kennedy's assassination, but who have no detailed knowledge of the facts of the assassination or of the many interpretations of those facts. By emphasising the less credible conspiracy theories, the media tries to discourage a sizeable part of the general public from exploring the subject.

E Was Oswald Standing in the Doorway?

The first published photograph of the JFK assassination shows the presidential limousine from the front, with President Kennedy visible through the windscreen reacting to his throat wound. In the background, part of the Texas School Book Depository can be seen. Among the spectators in the doorway of the building, just above and to the right of President Kennedy, is a man who looks remarkably like Lee Harvey Oswald.

The photograph in question was the fifth of seven taken at the time of the assassination by James 'Ike' Altgens, an Associated Press photographer. It is normally identified as Altgens no.6, after the pre–existing number under the image on the negative. The positions of the cars in the road, and the postures of the individuals within the cars, show that the photograph was taken at a point approximating to frame 255 of the Zapruder film, about three seconds before President Kennedy was hit in the head. According to the Warren Commission's case against Oswald, the only official suspect in the murder was elsewhere at this instant: 60 feet or 18 metres almost directly above the man in the photograph, aiming a rifle from the south–eastern corner window of the sixth floor of the TSBD.[1]

1. Several versions of the photograph can be found at http://www.jfkassassinationgallery.com/thumbnails.php?album=2. Frame 255 of the Zapruder film: http://www.assassinationresearch.com/zfilm/z255.jpg. For an account of James Altgens' experiences in Dealey Plaza, and a clear reproduction of his famous photograph, see Richard Trask, *Pictures of the Pain: Photography and the Assassination of President Kennedy*, Yeoman Press, 1994, pp.307–324.

The FBI quickly became aware that the photograph appeared to contradict the official verdict. Three days after the assassination, the Bureau spoke to Roy Truly, the superintendant of the TSBD, who pointed out that the man in the photograph looked like Billy Nolan Lovelady, a colleague of Lee Oswald's. Several other employees of the TSBD confirmed that Lovelady had been on the steps during or immediately before the assassination. William Shelley, Oswald's manager, stated that "as the Presidential Motorcade passed I was standing just outside the glass doors of the entrance ... Billy N. Lovelady ... was seated on the entrance steps just in front of me" and "several people were out there waiting to watch the motorcade and I went to join them.... Billy Lovelady joined us shortly afterwards ... just outside the glass doors there."[2] Sarah Stanton said that "I was standing on the front steps of the Texas School Book Depository with Mr. William Shelley ... and Billy Lovelady."[3] Billy Lovelady himself: "I happened to look on the outside and Mr. Shelley was standing outside with Miss Sarah Stanton, I believe her name is, and I said, 'Well, I'll go out there and talk with them, sit down and eat my lunch out there, set on the steps,' so I went out there."[4] Buell Wesley Frazier: "I was standing on the steps there ... I stayed around there pretty close to Mr. Shelley and this boy Billy Lovelady."[5] Harold Norman: "Billy Lovelady ... was sitting on the steps there."[6] James Jarman said that Lovelady was "standing on the stairway as you go out the front door."[7] Danny Garcia Arce stated that he went outside with Lovelady and Shelley: "I was standing in front of the Texas School Book Depository. I was on that grassy area part in front.... The other guys ... were all in front of the building." He identified Lovelady as the man in the photograph.[8] Virginia Rackley pointed out Billy Lovelady on Commission Exhibit 203, a copy of Altgens' photograph.[9] No–one claimed to have seen Oswald on the steps.

2. William Shelley: CE 1381, p.84 (*WCHE*, vol.22, p.673) and *WCHE*, vol.6, p.328.
3. Sarah Stanton: CE 1381, p.89 (*WCHE*, vol.22, p.675).
4. Billy Lovelady: *WCHE*, vol.6, p.338.
5. Buell Wesley Frazier: *WCHE*, vol.2, p.233.
6. Harold Norman: *WCHE*, vol.3, p.189.
7. James Jarman: *ibid.*, p.202.
8. Danny Garcia Arce: *WCHE*, vol.6, pp.365–367.
9. Virginia Rackley, who by the time of her Warren Commission deposition had become Mrs Donald Baker: *WCHE*, vol.7, p.515. CE 203: *WCHE*, vol.16, p.584.

The matter appeared to be settled: Billy Lovelady was the man in the photograph.

Although the facial features and hairline of the man in the photograph were consistent with both Oswald and Lovelady, the small size of the figure left ample room for ambiguity. The figure is less than half a millimetre wide on Altgens' negative, and occupies one per cent of the width of the frame. Critics of the Warren Commission pointed out that the evidence collected by the FBI was not definitive, and that the Commission's account of the issue was superficial. The Commission dealt with the matter very briefly. It published only poor quality versions of Altgens' photograph, and failed to publish comparison photographs of Oswald and Lovelady.[10] Altgens' photograph and other images and testimony suggest that there were perhaps fourteen people standing on or immediately in front of the steps during the assassination. Only three of them, Lovelady, Shelley and Frazier, were questioned by the Warren Commission about the identity of the man in the photograph. Frazier and Lovelady were each asked to mark CE 369, a copy of the photograph, with an arrow to indicate their positions, but the exhibit contains only one arrow.[11] One of the weaker criticisms was the observation that whereas Shelley and Norman had claimed that Lovelady had been sitting on the steps, the man in the photograph is standing. No doubt Lovelady sat on the steps to eat his lunch, and then stood up to watch the motorcade, as anyone surely must have done to see past the crowd standing three–deep on the sidewalk in front of the TSBD.

One of the early critics, Harold Weisberg, questioned the FBI's identification on other grounds. He noted that certain features of the shirt in the photograph matched the shirt Oswald was wearing when he was arrested: both shirts were torn, the top two or three buttons were undone, and other buttons were missing.[12]

10. Warren Commission's account: *WR*, pp.147–149 and p.644. For the poor quality of the photographs, see e.g. CE 900 (*WCHE*, vol.18, p.93).
11. Frazier: *WCHE*, vol.2, p.242. Lovelady: *WCHE*, vol.6, p.338. CE 369: *WCHE*, vol.16, p.965.
12. Harold Weisberg, *Whitewash II*, self–published, 1966, p.250. For the distinguishing features of Oswald's shirt, see *WCHE*, vol.21, pp.467–470. For a more recent version of Weisberg's argument that the man in the doorway was in fact Oswald, see David Wrone, *The Zapruder Film: Reframing JFK's Assassination*, University Press of Kansas, 2003, pp.174–180.

Against Weisberg, it was pointed out that Oswald's shirt had a different pattern to the shirt in Altgens' black–and–white photograph, which has a noticeable check pattern: medium–toned squares surrounded by distinct light and dark horizontal and vertical stripes. Oswald's shirt did not have a check pattern, but was a solid mid–brown with thin horizontal and vertical gold flecks. The question is complicated by the fact that Oswald may have changed his shirt between the assassination and his arrest.[13] Even if Oswald had changed his shirt, his original shirt would have been similar to the shirt he was wearing when arrested. Two witnesses mention a brown colour but no pattern.[14]

The matter was further confused by Lovelady himself. The FBI required a photographic record of Lovelady, and asked him to wear the shirt he had worn on the day of the assassination. Lovelady selected a shirt with short sleeves and wide vertical stripes,[15] rather than long sleeves and a check pattern like the shirt in Altgens' photograph. According to a journalist who had interviewed him, "Lovelady also said that on November 22 he was wearing a red–and–white striped sport shirt buttoned near the neck."[16] When Lovelady was informed of the discrepancy, he claimed that he had told the FBI that the short–sleeved shirt with the wide vertical stripes was not in fact the shirt he had worn on 22 November 1963, and that the actual shirt had long sleeves and a check pattern. He told CBS News: "Well, when the FBI took me in the shirt, I told them it wasn't the same shirt."[17]

Two films resolved the question of which shirt Billy Lovelady was wearing on the day of the assassination. A home movie, shot in colour by John Martin, was rediscovered in the 1970s. The film shows a crowd of people outside the main entrance of the TSBD a few minutes after the assassination. One of the people is unmistakeably Billy Lovelady. He is wearing a long–sleeved check

13. Changing his shirt: *WR*, p.622; and Handwritten notes of Captain J.W. Fritz's interview of Oswald, p.7.
14. Linnie Mae Randle: *WCHE*, vol.2, p.250; Marrion Baker: *WCHE*, vol.3, p.257.
15. Lovelady in his striped shirt: CD 457, addendum p.2.
16. *New York Herald Tribune*: *WCHE*, vol.22, p.793–794.
17. Quoted in Josiah Thompson, *Six Seconds in Dallas: A Micro–Study of the Kennedy Assassination*, Bernard Geis Associates, 1967, p.227. The House Select Committee on Assassinations included in its discussion of the issue a photograph of Lovelady in his check shirt: *HSCA Appendix*, vol.6, pp.286–293.

shirt with red squares and white and blue horizontal and vertical stripes. The colour film matched Altgens' black–and–white photograph. Billy Lovelady was clearly the man in the photograph. One trivial inconsistency remained. In Altgens' photograph, the top few buttons of Lovelady's shirt are undone. In most of the published still frames from Martin's film, taken just a few minutes later and showing Lovelady in profile, the shirt appears to be buttoned up almost to the collar. A viewing of the full film, however, shows that his check shirt was in fact open as Lovelady turned briefly to his left, revealing the white T–shirt that is visible in James Altgens' photograph. Another previously unknown film, taken a few minutes after 2pm by Charles Buck of WFAA–TV, showed Billy Lovelady in the police station just as the recently arrested Lee Oswald was led past him. This black–and–white film shows clearly that Lovelady was wearing a long–sleeved check shirt with the top few buttons undone, and a white T–shirt underneath.[18]

Photographic evidence proves definitively that at the time of the JFK assassination Billy Lovelady was wearing a long–sleeved check shirt open at the neck, over a white T–shirt. To almost all observers, that shirt matched the one worn by the figure in James Altgens' photograph. It is now generally agreed that the man on the front steps of the TSBD was Billy Nolan Lovelady, not Lee Harvey Oswald.

Several decades after the question had been settled, a discussion on an online forum raised the possibility that Lee Oswald may after all have been standing in the doorway of the Texas School Book Depository during the assassination.[19] In several frames of two news films taken by Dave Wiegman and Jimmy Darnell a matter of seconds after the assassination, a figure is visible in the western corner of the TSBD doorway. From the cameras' point of view, the figure is standing to the left of the man in the Altgens photograph who has been identified as Billy Lovelady. Although the figure in the films is insufficiently distinct to permit a definitive identifica-

18. For a clear frame from the Martin film, photographs of Oswald's and Lovelady's shirts, and a good reproduction of Altgens' image, see Robert Groden, *The Killing of a President*, Viking Penguin, 1993, pp.186–187. For an online comparison of the figure in the photograph and Lovelady, see http://www.spartacus.schoolnet.co.uk/JFKlovelady.htm.

19. http://educationforum.ipbhost.com/index.php?showtopic=20354.

tion, it appears to be a white man, dressed in a casual work shirt. The figure's posture has earned it the name 'Prayer Man'.

A process of elimination allows the possibility that Prayer Man may have been Oswald. Fourteen named witnesses are generally assumed to have been standing on or just in front of the TSBD steps. Of these fourteen, the seven women and two black men may be ruled out immediately. If the online contributors are to be believed, the remaining five white men may also be ruled out, with varying degrees of certainty. Joe Molina and William Shelley were each wearing a suit and tie, unlike the figure. Billy Lovelady can be identified standing to the east of the figure. Buell Wesley Frazier was wearing a jacket, unlike the figure, and testified that he was standing to the east of Shelley and Lovelady. Otis Williams testified that he was standing at the eastern end of the steps, a location supported by Molina's testimony. Williams's clothing is undetermined, but his job title, Bookkeeping Supervisor, suggests that he would not have worn a casual shirt to work.

Prayer Man's location, at the top of the steps with his back to the glass door, implies that he is unlikely to have been a passer–by. He is more likely to have been someone who worked inside the TSBD building, as were all the fourteen named witnesses assumed to have been standing in the doorway during the assassination. All of the TSBD's white, male, manual workers were accounted for, apart from Oswald.

Against the notion that the man was Oswald is the fact that no–one in the vicinity of the doorway is on record identifying Oswald at the time of the shooting. Billy Lovelady specifically denied having seen Oswald after they stopped work more than half an hour before the assassination.[20]

At the time of writing, the only copies of the Darnell and Wiegman films in public circulation are of relatively poor quality. It is possible that better–quality versions will allow Oswald to be definitively eliminated either as the figure in the doorway or as the gunman on the sixth floor.

20. Billy Lovelady: *WCHE*, vol.6, p.338.

Bibliography

Report of the President's Commission on the Assassination of President John F. Kennedy, US Government Printing Office, 1964.

Hearings before the President's Commission on the Assassination of President John F. Kennedy, US Government Printing Office, 1964.

Alfred G. Olivier and Arthur J. Dziemian, *Wound Ballistics of 6.5–mm Mannlicher–Carcano Ammunition*, Chemical Research and Development Laboratories Report 3264, NARA.

CIA Inspector General, *Report on Plots to Assassinate Fidel Castro*, 1967, NARA RIF no. 104–10213–10101.

Interim Report of the Senate Select Committee to Study Governmental Operations with Respect to Intelligence Activities: Assassination Plots Involving Foreign Leaders, US Government Printing Office, 1975.

Final Report of the Senate Select Committee to Study Governmental Operations with Respect to Intelligence Activities, Book V: The Investigation of the Assassination of President John F. Kennedy: Performance of Intelligence Agencies, US Government Printing Office, 1976.

Final Report of the Select Committee on Assassinations, US Government Printing Office, 1979.

National Research Council, *Report of the Committee on Ballistic Acoustics*, report no. PB83–218461, 1982.

Foreign Relations of the United States, 1961–1963, US Government Printing Office, 1997.

Don Adams, *From an Office Building with a High–Powered Rifle*, Trine Day, 2012.

Gary Aguilar, 'The Converging Medical Case for Conspiracy in the Death of JFK,' in James Fetzer, ed., *Murder in Dealey Plaza: What We Know Now That We Didn't Know Then About The Death of JFK*, Catfeet Press, 2000, pp.175–217.

Gary Aguilar, 'Is Vincent Bugliosi Right that Neutron Activation Analysis Proves Oswald's Guilt?' at http://www.maryferrell.org/wiki/index.php/Essay_-_Is_Vincent_Bugliosi_Right_that_Neutron_Activation_Analysis_Proves_Oswalds_Guilt.

Gary Aguilar and Josiah Thompson, 'The Magic Bullet: Even More Magical Than We Knew' at http://history-matters.com/essays/frameup/EvenMoreMagical/EvenMoreMagical.htm.

Gary Aguilar and Kathy Cunningham, 'How Five Investigations into JFK's Medical/Autopsy Evidence Got it Wrong,' at http://www.history-matters.com/essays/jfkmed/How5Investigations/How5InvestigationsGotItWrong.htm.

Luis A. Alvarez, 'A Physicist Examines the Kennedy Assassination Film', *American Journal of Physics*, vol.44 no.9 (September 1976), pp.813–27, reproduced at *HSCA Appendix*, vol.1, pp.428–441.

Sheldon Appleton, 'The Mystery of the Kennedy Assassination: What the American Public Believes,' *The Public Perspective*, October/November 1998, pp.13–17.

Desmond Ball, *Politics and Force Levels: The Strategic Missile Program of the Kennedy Administration*, University of California Press, 1980.

Jan Knippers Black, *United States Penetration of Brazil*, University of Pennsylvania Press, 1977.

Robert Blakey and Richard Billings, *The Plot to Kill the President*, NYT Books, 1981.

William Blum, *Killing Hope: US Military and CIA Interventions Since World War II*, Common Courage Press, 1995.

Steve Bocham, 'Understanding Silvia Odio: What the LaFontaines Don't Tell You,' *Kennedy Assassination Chronicles*, vol.2, issue 2 (Summer 1996), pp.28–31.

Rex Bradford, 'The Fourteen Minute Gap,' at http://www.history-matters.com/essays/frameup/FourteenMinuteGap/FourteenMinuteGap.htm.

Madeleine Brown, *Texas in the Morning*, Conservatory Press, 1997.

William A. Buckingham, *Operation Ranch Hand: The Air Force and Herbicides in Southeast Asia*, US Government Printing Office, 1982.

Michael Calder, *JFK vs CIA: The Central Intelligence Agency's Assassination of the President*, West LA Publishers, 1998.

Darren K. Carlson, 'Most Americans Believe Oswald Conspired With Others to Kill JFK,' at http://www.gallup.com/poll/1813/most-americans-believe-oswald-conspired-others-kill-jfk.aspx.

G. Paul Chambers, *Head Shot: The Science Behind the JFK Assassination*, Prometheus Books, 2010.

Noam Chomsky and Howard Zinn, ed., *The Pentagon Papers*, Senator Gravel Edition, Beacon Press, 1972, vol.4.

Noam Chomsky, *Rethinking Camelot: JFK, the Vietnam War, and US Political Culture*, South End Press, 1993.

George de Mohrenschildt, ed. Michael Rinella, *Lee Harvey Oswald As I Knew Him*, University Press of Kansas, 2014.

James DiEugenio, *Destiny Betrayed: JFK, Cuba and the Garrison Case*, 2nd edition, Skyhorse Publishing, 2012.

James Douglass, *JFK and the Unspeakable: Why He Died and Why It Matters*, Orbis Books, 2008.

Edward Epstein, *Inquest: the Warren Commission and the Establishment of Truth*, Viking Press, 1966.

Barry Ernest, *The Girl on the Stairs: My Search for a Missing Witness to the Assassination of John F. Kennedy*, Createspace, 2011.

James Fetzer, ed., *The Great Zapruder Film Hoax: Deceit and Deception in the Death of JFK*, Catfeet Press, 2003.

Roger Feinman, *Between the Signal and the Noise*, unpublished manuscript.

Harold Feldman, 'Fifty–One Witnesses,' *Minority of One*, March 1965.

Gaeton Fonzi, *The Last Investigation*, Thunder's Mouth Press, 1993.

Ron Friedrich, 'Ed Hoffman's Changing Story,' *Kennedy Assassination Chronicles*, vol.1 issue 2 (June 1995), pp.31–32.

Stewart Galanor, *Cover–Up*, Kestrel Books, 1998.

James K. Galbraith, 'Exit Strategy,' *Boston Review*, October–November 2003.

Raymond L. Garthoff, *Reflections on the Cuban Missile Crisis*, Brookings Institution, 1989.

Paul C. Giannelli, 'Comparative Bullet Lead Analysis: A Retrospective,' *Criminal Law Bulletin*, vol.47 no.2 (September 2011), pp.306–315.

William Conrad Gibbons, ed., *The US Government and the Vietnam War: Executive and Legislative Roles and Relationships, Part 2 (1961–64)*, Princeton University Press, 1986.

Michael D. Glascock, 'Overview of Neutron Activation Analysis' at http://archaeometry.missouri.edu/naa_overview.html.

Earl Golz, 'SS Imposters Spotted by JFK Witnesses,' *Dallas Morning News*, 27 August 1978, p.1A.

Joel Grant, 'Body Snatchers at Love Field?' at http://mcadams.posc.mu.edu/b_snatch.htm.

Ian Griggs, 'The Paper Bag that Never Was, part 1,' *Dealey Plaza Echo*, vol.1, no.1, July 1996, pp.30–36.

Ian Griggs, 'The Paper Bag that Never Was, part 2,' *Dealey Plaza Echo*, vol.1, no.2, November 1996, pp.30–38.

Robert Groden, *The Killing of a President*, Viking Studio Press, 1993.

Robert Groden, *The Search for Lee Harvey Oswald*, Viking Penguin, 1995.

David Halberstam, *The Best and the Brightest*, Random House, 1972.

Warren Hinckle and William Turner, *The Fish is Red: The Story of the Secret War Against Castro*, Harper and Row, 1981.

Ed Hoffman with Ron Friedrich, *Eye Witness*, JFK Lancer, 1997.

Henry Hurt, *Reasonable Doubt: An Investigation into the Assassination of John F. Kennedy*, Henry Holt, 1985.

Michael James, 'Lawsuit is settled in favor of former Secret Service agent; book claimed man accidentally fired bullet that killed Kennedy,' *Baltimore Sun*, 3 February 1998.

Joachim Joesten, *The Dark Side of Lyndon Baines Johnson*, Peter Dawn Ltd, 1968.

Barb Junkkarinen, 'First Shot / First Hit Circa Z–190,' *Kennedy Assassination Chronicles*, vol.5 no.2 (Summer 1999), pp.24–28.

Michael L. Kurtz, 'Lee Harvey Oswald in New Orleans: a Reappraisal,' *Louisiana History*, vol.21 no.1 (Winter 1980), pp.7–22.

Michael L. Kurtz, *Crime of the Century: The Kennedy Assassination from a Historian's Perspective*, 2nd edition, University of Tennessee Press, 1993.

M. Duke Lane, 'Freeway Man,' at http://mcadams.posc.mu.edu/freewayman.htm.

A.J. Langguth, *Hidden Terrors: The Truth about US Police Operations in Latin America*, Pantheon Books, 1978.

Yasha Levine, 'A People's History of Koch Industries: How Stalin Funded the Tea Party Movement,' at http://exiledonline.com/a-peoples-history-of-koch-industries-how-stalin-funded-the-tea-party-movement/.

David Lifton, *Best Evidence: Disguise and Deception in the Assassination of John F. Kennedy*, Macmillan, 1980.

R. Linsker, R.L. Garwin, H. Chernoff, P. Horowitz, and N.F. Ramsey, 'Synchronization of the Acoustic Evidence in the Assassination of President Kennedy,' *Science & Justice*, vol.45 no.4 (October 2005), pp.207–226.

Charles Maechling, Jr., 'The Murderous Mind of the Latin American Military,' *Los Angeles Times*, 18 March 1982, part 2, p.11.

Andrew M. Mason, 'Witness Evidence in the JFK Assassination,' at http://www.spmlaw.ca/jfk/shot_pattern_evidence.pdf.

Steve McGonigle and Jennifer Emily, '18 Dallas County Cases Overturned by DNA Relied Heavily on Eyewitness Testimony,' *Dallas Morning News*, 12 October 2008.

Gerald D. McKnight, *Breach of Trust: How the Warren Commission Failed the Nation and Why*, University Press of Kansas, 2005.

Philip Melanson, 'Hidden Exposure: Cover–Up and Intrigue in the CIA: Secret Possession of the Zapruder Film,' *The Third Decade*, vol.1 no.1 (November 1984), pp.13–21.

David W. Mantik, 'Paradoxes of the JFK Assassination: The Medical Evidence Decoded,' in James Fetzer, ed., *Murder in Dealey Plaza: What We Know Now That We Didn't Know Then About The Death of JFK*, Catfeet Press, 2000, pp.219–297.

Sylvia Meagher, *Accessories After the Fact: the Warren Commission, the Authorities, and the Report*, Bobbs–Merrill, 1967.

Bonar Menninger, *Mortal Error: The Shot That Killed JFK*, St. Martin's Press, 1992.

Clark R. Mollenhoff, *Despoilers of Democracy*, Doubleday, 1965.

Jefferson Morley, 'What Jane Roman Said, part 3' at http://www.history-matters.com/essays/frameup/WhatJaneRomanSaid/WhatJaneRomanSaid_3.htm.

Jefferson Morley, 'What Jane Roman Said, part 6,' at http://www.history-matters.com/essays/frameup/WhatJaneRomanSaid/WhatJaneRomanSaid_6.htm.

Morris H. Morley, *Imperial State and Revolution: The United States and Cuba, 1952–1986*, Cambridge University Press, 1987.

W.R. Morris, *The Men Behind the Guns*, Angel Lea Books, 1975.

Martha Moyer, 'Ordering the Rifle,' *Kennedy Assassination Chronicles*, vol.2 no.1 (March 1996), pp.23–31.

Fred T. Newcomb and Perry Adams, 'Did Someone Alter the Medical Evidence?', *Skeptic*, Special Issue no.9 (September–October 1975), pp.24–27.

John Newman, *JFK and Vietnam: Deception, Intrigue, and the Struggle for Power*, Warner Books, 1992.

John Newman, *Oswald and the CIA*, Carroll and Graf, 1995.

Mark North, *Act of Treason: The Role of J. Edgar Hoover in the Assassination of President Kennedy*, Skyhorse Publishing, 1991.

Thomas P. O'Neill, Jr., *Man of the House: The Life and Political Memoirs of Speaker Tip O'Neill*, Random House, 1987.

Milton E. Osborne, *Strategic Hamlets in South Vietnam: A Survey and a Comparison*, Cornell University Southeast Asia Program Publications, 1970.

Michael Parenti, *The Assassination of Julius Caesar: A People's History of Ancient Rome*, The New Press, 2003.

Thomas G. Paterson, ed., *Kennedy's Quest for Victory: American Foreign Policy, 1961–1963*, Oxford University Press, 1989.

Thomas Powers and Alan Rich, 'Robbing the Grave,' *New York Magazine*, February 23, 1981.

John Prados, 'JFK and the Diem Coup' at http://www.gwu.edu/~nsarchiv/NSAEBB/NSAEBB101/.

L. Fletcher Prouty, *JFK: The CIA, Vietnam and the Plot to Assassinate John F. Kennedy*, Citadel Press, 2003.

Stephen G. Rabe, *The Most Dangerous Area in the World: John F. Kennedy Confronts Communist Revolution in Latin America*, University of North Carolina Press, 1999.

Erik Randich and Patrick M. Grant, 'Proper Assessment of the JFK Assassination Bullet Lead Evidence from Metallurgical and Statistical Perspectives,' *Journal of Forensic Sciences*, vol.51 no.4 (July 2006), pp.717–728.

Dan Robertson, *Definitive Proof: The Secret Service Murder of President John Fitzgerald Kennedy*, Lulu.com, 2006.

Howard Roffman, *Presumed Guilty: How and Why the Warren Commission Framed Lee Harvey Oswald*, Fairleigh Dickinson University Press, 1975.

Bertrand Russell, '16 Questions on the Assassination,' *Minority of One*, 6 September 1964, pp.6–8.

David Scheim, *Contract on America: The Mafia Murder of President John F. Kennedy*, Zebra, 1989.

Daniel Schulman, *Sons of Wichita: How the Koch Brothers Became America's Most Powerful and Private Dynasty*, Grand Central Publishing, 2014.

Peter Dale Scott, *Deep Politics and the Death of JFK*, University of California Press, 1993.

Bill Simpich, *State Secret: Wiretapping in Mexico City, Double Agents, and the Framing of Lee Oswald*, at http://www.maryferrell.org/wiki/index.php/State_Secret_Preface.

Cliff Spiegelman, William A. Tobin, William D. James, Simon J. Sheather, Stuart Wexler and D. Max Roundhill, 'Chemical and Forensic Analysis of JFK Assassination Bullet Lots: Is a Second Shooter Possible?', *The Annals of Applied Statistics*, vol.1 no.2 (2007), pp.287–301.

Michael A. Stroscio, 'More Physical Insight into the Assassination of President Kennedy,' *Physics and Society*, vol.25 no.4 (October 1996), pp.7–8.

Thomas P. Sullivan, 'Police Experiences with Recording Custodial Interrogations,' *Judicature*, vol.88 no.3 (November–December 2004), pp.132–136.

Anthony Summers, *Not In Your Lifetime: The Assassination of JFK*, Headline, 2013.

Donald Thomas, 'Echo Correlation Analysis and the Acoustic Evidence in the Kennedy Assassination Revisited,' *Science & Justice*, vol.41 no.1 (January 2001), pp.21–32.

Donald Thomas, *Hear No Evil: Social Constructivism and the Forensic Evidence in the Kennedy Assassination*, Mary Ferrell Foundation Press, 2010.

Josiah Thompson, *Six Seconds in Dallas: A Micro–Study of the Kennedy Assassination*, Bernard Geis Associates, 1967.

Josiah Thompson, 'Bedrock Evidence in the Kennedy Assassination,' at http://www.maryferrell.org/wiki/index.php/Essay_-_Bedrock_Evidence_in_the_Kennedy_Assassination.

Richard Trask, *Pictures of the Pain: Photography and the Assassination of President Kennedy*, Yeoman Press, 1994.

Richard J. Walton, *Cold War and Counter–Revolution: The Foreign Policy of John F. Kennedy*, Viking Press, 1972.

Cyril H. Wecht, 'A Critique of President Kennedy's Autopsy,' in Josiah Thompson, *Six Seconds in Dallas: A Micro–Study of the Kennedy Assassination*, Bernard Geis Associates, 1967, pp.278–284.

Harold Weisberg, *Whitewash: the Report on the Warren Report*, Weisberg, 1965.

Harold Weisberg, *Whitewash II*, Weisberg, 1966.

Harold Weisberg, *Post Mortem: JFK Assassination Cover–Up Smashed*, Weisberg, 1975.

Harold Weisberg, *Never Again*, Carroll and Graf, 1995.

Harold Weisberg, *Autopsy of a JFK Assassination Best Seller: Best Evidence as Bad Evidence*, unpublished manuscript.

Charles Wilber, *Medicolegal Investigation of the President John F. Kennedy Murder*, Charles C. Thomas, 1978.

Mary Woodward, 'Witness From the News Describes Assassination,' *Dallas Morning News*, 23 November 1963, p.3.

David Wrone, *The Zapruder Film: Reframing JFK's Assassination*, University Press of Kansas, 2003.

Roland Zavada, *Analysis of Selected Motion Picture Photographic Evidence*, Kodak Technical Report, Eastman Kodak, 1998.

Howard Zinn, *SNCC: The New Abolitionists*, Beacon Press, 1964.

Index

Printed in Great Britain
by Amazon

31525172R00115